My Fathers House

"A conversational journey to reclaim and behold the restoration of the community that Jesus gave his life for."

No part of this book may be used or reproduced for financial gain for anyone other than BreadStone. However, reproduction is granted to less than one hundred words at a time for whosoever needs the information for the education of the house hold of Christian faith.

Copyright 2021 © by Robert A. Foster All rights reserved.

ISBN-13 978-1737773306
Library of Congress 1-10750202051

Final layout and cover by Robert A. Foster

Printed in the United States of America
Set mostly in 13pt. Palatino.

WWW.BreadstonePublishing.Com

All Scriptures used;
NASB, New American Standard Bible.
WET, Wuest Expanded Translation.

"So then, while we have opportunity, let us do good to all people, and especially to those who are of the household of the faith" ~ Galatians 6:10 NASB.

To the the faces long gone,
still present and yet to be greeted...

Introduction

Chapter One - Taking the rose colored glasses off?
Chapter Two - The Pernicious Plan.
Chapter Three - Evil in the Modern Age.
Chapter four - Whispers of the Promised Land.
Chapter Five - Fire of Spirituality.
Chapter Six - My Father's House
Chapter Seven - The Mighty Three, My Protection Be.

Questions

Introduction

It is somewhat traditional within modern book publishing to include an "about page" at the end of the book concerning the background of the author. It is often short, only a few paragraphs and is often in my case made to be slightly entertaining.

But, because of the nature of this book, and because I am at the core a storyteller I see no possible way for me to separate my personal journey from the basic message of this book and the ones that may follow in this vein. Therefore, I am not even going to try.

There is also a basic tradition in many places within the Body of Christ to give your testimony before delivering any teachings or sermons. This is a good tradition because it helps to build a connection with each other, promoting trust and bonding within the community.

So in the next few pages I would like to introduce myself to you, not for self-promotion or to get you to donate to some cause or bank account, but for you to get an idea of my background and thinking as you ponder my words in the rest of the book.

Therefore, if you have serious problems with the Charismatic, Vineyard movement, Celtic Christianity, Prophetic, Christian music, signs & wonders, house church, or anything related to those topics, I would suggest you either put this book back on the bookshelf you got it from. Or if you have already bought the book and you have changed your mind, then please consider donating it to a good used bookstore for another to find. Because, most likely the Holy Spirit has not yet prepared the soil of your heart for you to listen. But if your problems with these groups and movements are like mine, seeing what they *could* be, yet aggravated at how far away they are from what they *should* be! Then keep reading because it's that "unsettled" feeling that the Holy Spirit is using within you to pray for change.

It should also be noted that I will often be referencing music from various Christian music artists of the past as well as the present. That is because they have often been a source of encouragement, uplifting and teaching that the Holy Spirit has used with me. Most of these songs can be found on any of the modern music platforms, so please consider looking them up for yourself and perhaps their music videos to rediscover the message for yourself. Also, if you're looking for a standard 'teaching' book, highly structured with bullet points and enough footnotes to choke a horse, then you might want to just wander on. Not only is that not me anymore, but after the Lord took me down the road of discovery of my heritage coming from the shores of Northumbria at the edge of Celtic lands. I find that as I bend into the Celtic concepts of conversational teaching far better, and that suits me fine. This book is a journey and exploration and therefore it is written in a conversational form.

Finally, I am under no illusion that what is contained within this book will be well accepted by the general Christian world. In fact I suspect many, especially in the leadership world of the Charismatic will be outright angered. I am not sorry for exposing the darkness, I just wish someone had done it twenty years before. But this book is not really written for them, for their approval. It's for the lost, hurt, and lonely forever residing in silence, within the corners of a broken system. But as an old friend of mine, Michael R. Carter, long dead, once said, "truth comforts the afflicted but afflicts the comfortable."

The Father has a home for you.

~Robert A. Foster

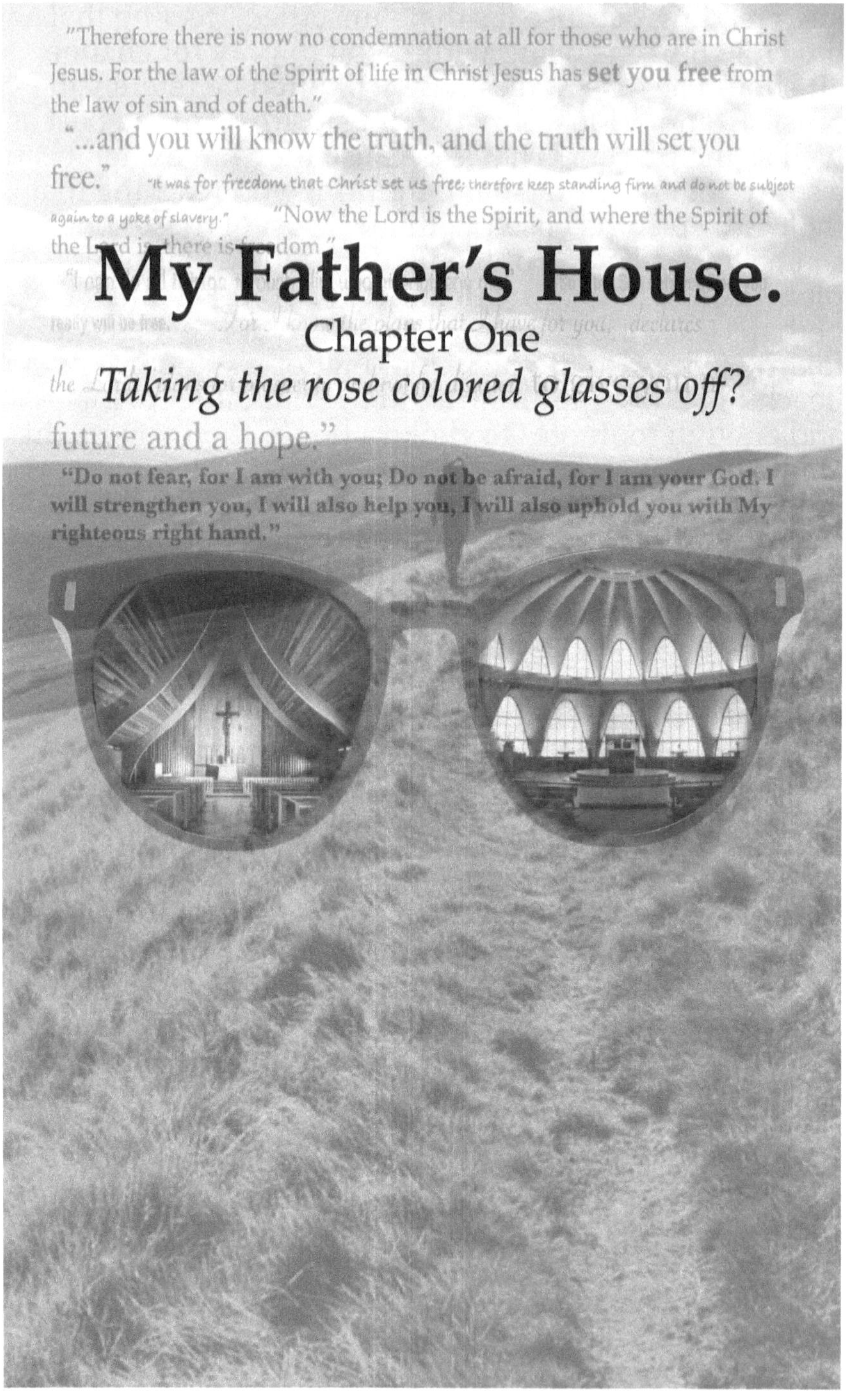

"Therefore there is now no condemnation at all for those who are in Christ Jesus. For the law of the Spirit of life in Christ Jesus has **set you free** from the law of sin and of death."

"...and you will know the truth, and the truth will set you free." *"It was for freedom that Christ set us free; therefore keep standing firm and do not be subject again to a yoke of slavery."* "Now the Lord is the Spirit, and where the Spirit of the Lord is, there is freedom."

My Father's House.
Chapter One
Taking the rose colored glasses off?

"Do not fear, for I am with you; Do not be afraid, for I am your God. I will strengthen you, I will also help you, I will also uphold you with My righteous right hand."

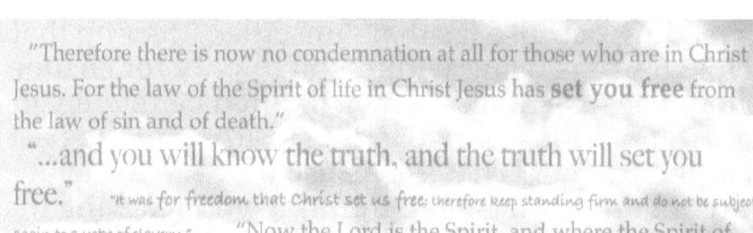

3

Margaret Becker – Who Am I?

"Who am I, Jesus, that You call me by name?
I am counting the stars, on Your blackened sky.
You call them all by name, You know them all by sight.
In this sea of lights, I sense Your majesty.
And I break at the thought that One so great,
could care for me..."

The question "who am I?" is an ongoing, ever-expanding question that often flows back and forth depending on, as it says later on in the song, "The Storms of Life."

The Apostle Paul counted all things as loss at one point. Yet, he still made a point of telling some of his backstory. Not for bragging, but for connection, for the community he was writing to.

My life started in the mid-1960's, in the Southwest, as the youngest child of a traveling coal miner. In time, he left that life to get a job in the Pacific Northwest. So, fast forward through many winter storms, wet summers, mud boots, sheep shearing, filling hay wagons in the summer sun, and unofficial high school activities that could have landed me and others in jail.

I came to Christ after graduating from High School. There was no one around, no one sat me down to give me the "four spiritual laws." I simply found a book from Hal Lindsey that looked like a science fiction book called, "The Late Great Planet Earth."

Sitting on a dock, alone under the stars, I made a decision and talked to God for the first time in my life. The words were not complicated, eloquent, or well thought out. In fact I had searched five times, page by page to find the prayer for salvation at the end of the book. I could not find it, so I just "faked it" and made up my own based on what I remembered. That little fact of making it up as I go has become the 'hallmark' of my Spiritual walk to this day. God has always discouraged me away from the "form" to follow the life. Not that there have not been times that I have not tried to follow the "form" but as I look back, I realize it never really had any life, only a legalistic illusion.

I shortly thereafter landed in a small Baptist church of mostly elderly senior citizens. After six months of trying to wrap my head around the new Christian terminology and ways of doing things, I was starting to think I had taken a serious detour in my life as I watched the hidden hypocrisy.

At this point I had already decided that this new "religious life" was a bad step and I needed at some point to just walk away. What I was reading in the Bible seemed so very far away from the reality of the lives I was watching around me. This is because, even though I knew almost nothing at this point, it just seemed logical to me that if you're going to be a Christian, and the Bible is your guide, you should be following it.

It was also during this time that I was doing my level best to assimilate the Christian songs on the local radio station. At one point I heard an advertisement on the radio for a conference across the border in Canada called, "Teach us to Pray."

A day or so later I was at a friend's house playing "Risk" when the pastor of the Baptist church stopped in. He had been attending the conference and was really excited. The pastor was doing his best to encourage us to join him the next time because it was the "free night" and you did not need to pay to get in.

My friend seemed mildly excited and I gave it friendly lip service to appease the room, knowing that I had no intention of ever attending.

The next day, my mind had totally forgotten the night before when my friend called, inviting me to join him in Canada. Without thinking, without even trying to stop myself, I suddenly found myself saying "Yes" to his request. All the while wondering after he hung up, "why did I do that?"

Many years ago I heard a well known speaker refer to God as 'Jehovah-sneaky.' And sneaky He has always been with me. Amy Grant has a song called, "1974."

This song for me has become like a memorial of that special moment in my life.

Amy Grant, "1974"
"We were young and none of us knew quite what to say
But the feeling moved among us in silence anyway
Slowly we had made,
quite a change--
Somewhere we had crossed a big line
Down upon our knees,
we had tasted Holy Wine.
And no one could sway us in a life time.

Purer than the sky, behind the rain
Falling down all around us
Calling out from a boundless love.
Love had lit a fire; we were the flame

Burning into the darkness, shining out from inside us.
Not a word.
And no one had to say we were changed.
Nothing else we lived through would ever be same the same.
Knowing the truth that we had gained."

    In 1984 we attended the last session of the "Teach us to Pray" Vineyard conference taught by John Wimber. I feel I could write an entire chapter of the events that took place, or at least many paragraphs. But as you have most likely guessed, this one event impacted me in a profound way, catapulting me down a path that has now lasted for well over 30 years.
    The power of His presence, the Holy Spirit fell on me, forever changing my life. Crazy wild stuff took place that was so "over the top" compared to my very limited Christian experience of six months that I realized that I had been looking at the church and not Him, Jesus Christ. I was looking with the wrong glasses, evaluating God according to the church, not the other way around.
    I remember standing next to my friend in the meeting,

we were singing these new upbeat worship songs. Then at one point during worship I realized even with our eyes closed we were singing them perfectly as if we already knew all the words, even after each song changed.

Turning my head I mentioned it to him and we were both amazed. It was shortly after that, someone in one of the many metal folding chairs at the end of our row fell and his chair made a big noise as it crashed into something else. Honest to God, my first thought when I turned my head and looked down the long row to see him on the floor was very disapproving, "What a light weight!" I said to myself. This thought was most likely influenced by my drinking past as I was one of the few in my High School who could not only drink a bottle of tequila by myself, but keep functioning as well.

One by one, every few moments another person fell in our row, making a big crash. Then at some point, my mind registered that whatever was happening, it was coming my way. This one thought shot my fear level up though the roof. Panicked, I was determined that whatever it was, I was going to do everything I could to ignore it and try and focus everything I had, into worship. With each person going down in the line, it became harder to ignore the approaching unknown that was drawing near.

At one point I realized something happened and I turned my head expecting to see my friend. Looking down, I found him kneeling on the floor and my first thought was "oh no, it's got him!" Shooting my head back forward, I tried harder to focus, to block out what was happening. Then suddenly a hand was slammed into my back. Twisting my head around to the people behind me, I clearly saw someone who was more than one row back, being held up as this person stretched their hand out to reach me. That person, to this day I don't know if it was male or female, but this person looked like they were body surfing at a rock concert. And out of their mouth yelled, "Receive the Holy Spirit!" And that... was the last thing I remembered.

To this day I have no idea how much time passed. All I know is that when I came to, I was standing and not on the floor like everyone else with my hands up in the air. Lowering my arms, I could clearly see the worship band was in the process of packing up to leave. I started to look around and noticed my friend was also starting to wake up from his position of kneeling on the floor. We talked, clueless as to what happened. Then with the encouragement of our pastor who arrived, we decided to walk around and learn whatever we could. Having been near the front we were totally unaware of the unfolding events behind us.

It was a shock, at least for myself, to see the inside of Vancouver's Agrodome behind us. It looked to my eyes like some sort of reverse bomb went off. Instead of pushing outwards like a normal bomb, this pulled everything inwards. Folding chairs were in heaps, people laid the floor some moving, most not. Off to the side was a long row of empty wheelchairs with a cluster of small children ministering at one end. With no adults present they were laying on hands, praying as the people cried and eventually the wheelchair bound got up to walk away.

Stepping over and around the people on the floor, we eventually made our way almost to the back when suddenly a bizarre sound filled with rage burst forth from the back of the room. Many people quickly moved towards the sound as both of us knew, down deep inside of us, that the sound had come from a demon. The rest of that night was filled with this kind of activity. And we participated in more than one healing or casting out that night.

But for the most part it was like ***Amy Grant's*** song, **"1974"**
"Slowly we had made, quite a change-- Somewhere we had crossed a big line.
Down upon our knees, we had tasted Holy Wine.
And no one could sway us in a life time."

That night I saw many things happen, eyes open, ears hear, people walk by the prayers of children. And to this day, I have never been the same.

Days moved into weeks and eventually the seasons changed. The little Baptist church grew as I kept getting invited over for dinner in one house after another. Telling my story as well as others stories I collected along the way. I now realize that the three of us that attended that night, all without any real planning took on various jobs. One preached, another taught, and I told stories. In time, the seventy some-odd people of this church grew to around two hundred as stories of healings started to happen within our own walls.

That event was the door that opened, a door that never really shut. Even though at times over the years I felt like I could not find it.

As the next few years marched along, a lot took place. I had a season of "strange" spiritual stuff take place. Intense visions during the day, so vivid, so real, that I had no idea what to do with them. Demonic attacks during the day and night that tried to kill me.

Sudden insights into every detail of a person's life, as well as walking into the church on Sundays, knowing what the pastor was going to preach before he delivered it. It was like a big door opened and I was reading everything, whether I wanted to know it or not. All these and more started making matters worse for myself, my spiritual experiences were now slipping into a realm beyond what others were experiencing.

For the little growing church, it had started to become normal to hear or experience healings or even the prophetic within its walls. But I quickly realized from my interactions with people that if I told them what was happening to me, I soon found myself on the "outside."

Silence seemed to be the solution as I soon found out from one particular event. I had suddenly become aware of the dark painful details of one person's life who attended this church. Overwhelmed by the information I now had in my mind, I sought out the council of an Elder of the church wanting to know what

I should do. The news I gave him had apparently overwhelmed him, and then by extension it did the same with his wife when he shared it to her. Unfortunately, it only took that one person, the elder's wife, who accidentally delivered the news directly to the person the information was about.

On that day, not only did everything explode and turn into a mess, but I
realized there was no one I could trust for council, for help. Full of pain, I made a decision to leave that church, but the Lord stopped me. For the next few years I lived in silence and only shared the "smaller things."

Years slipped by, I got married, the Lord prophetically arranged that. All the major spiritual stuff slowed to a stop and in time even the lesser prophetic soon followed.

Then one day an elderly man from Oregon entered the church. He was controversial in all that he did and as soon as he saw me he pointed right at me and declared that "I was the one, and the Lord sent him to train me." I attended his meetings and in that room with other people, it quickly became obvious that his attention was often directed only at me. He "awoke the dormant things within me and I started seeing things again." This went on for months until one day I dropped by Dwight's house after work. It was during this time he started to really share things that were now way over the top, even for me. For he was starting to tell me some of the hidden details about me and what the Lord was calling me to.

At this point everything within me rebelled. As far as I was concerned this dude had lost it and he was now bouncing off the Ozone. I dropped all contact with the guy and got as much distance from him as I could.
Time passed and at one point it was reported to me that Dwight closed up his small wood shop and moved back to Mt. Angel, Oregon. Life for myself moved on, I worked many jobs, and left the Baptist church to attend a new Vineyard church plant. Then after a series of God events, we returned to the Baptist church to find it had

fallen from the level we knew as it gained a new pastor that had no intention of pursuing the "things of the Spirit." A couple more years rolled by and after much "encouragement" from the Holy Spirit we left to start Church planting.

It was during these days a connection was built between myself and a group of local pastors. Our little house church that had no name, for the first time in several months gained one after a period of fasting. The Lord gave it the name, "My Father's House."

Like all new church planters with stars in their eyes, I envisioned a wild new future with levels of continual expansion planned in. We soon built a reputation among some of the pastors I met with. They would come to visit as an outside speaker, we would then minister prophetically, the power of the Holy Spirit would often come over them, making them cry as we brought healing to their souls.

It was during the early years of this planting project that a trusted intercessor suggested I get to know more about a larger prophetic ministry on the East Coast. One thing led to another and I felt I should join their Fellowship of Ministries. When I finally sent in the application something odd happened. The closer I got to the mailbox, the more I started to tremble. I finally managed to get it in the box and when I did, I heard the Spirit say, "your destiny is now in my hands."

It took one year to the date before I was accepted into the fellowship. But during that time our little church plant had a lot of fun, did a lot of things. During the last year and a half, the Lord really started the process of changing my thinking about the church plant. I would make a plan, prepare a message, and then pray that God would interrupt and do whatever He wanted.

As a result I carried the same unused sermon for over a year because the Lord never disappointed us. It was not uncommon for our meetings to last all day, sharing a meal together, worshiping, laughing and doing whatever we felt the Lord was leading us to. As a result, no one wanted to go home.

It was during these days I got a couple of profound dreams concerning this ministry I was joining. One dream was insight into some of the problems within the organization. It was strong enough that I questioned the Lord, "why do you want me to join that mess?"

The answer He quickly gave back was, "Because I needed to learn!" Then to my surprise, the Lord tossed my wife and I a curve ball through a prophetic word from one of our trusted intercessors. The next thing we knew, we were selling our small farm and moving across the state to a "land we did not know."

To sell our farm required us to put in a new well and that was money we did not have. Making a deal with the well driller to pay them after the sale of the land, we moved forward. God opened one door after another and after the well was drilled the cost was $5,555.00. When the land sold we paid the bill with the acquired interest off at $7,777.00. *It was God's grace to go and He had made all things complete.*

My Fathers House eventually shut down after we left as we started the process of planting a new church in a new land. But through rebellion, rejection, and witchcraft that project in time bottomed out and whimpered to death. A bit stressed out, a prophetic word came to us from a minister in Kansas, "You have always been a person who wants his ducks in a row. This time you do not get to have it. So move out!" This word was nearly word for word of the prophetic word we got several years before, so we knew it was time to leave. And according to the dreams I was getting, I knew we were moving to South Carolina to work for the same ministry I was a member of.

We sold in the middle of winter when nothing was selling. Loaded up all we could carry, equaling about twenty percent of what we owned and headed out. Stopping off at some friends after discovering we were badly over weight, we dropped off nearly a thousand pounds of books and food. Much of it went to a small Russian house church in Oregon, it was then that I realized the Lord was symbolically saying that he was going to purge our old ways of thinking (books, some over a hundred years old) and our old ways of providing (food we had stored from the farm)

To my surprise I got hired into the same department that for years I had problems with: distribution. I started out in data entry, and after seven years in the Carolinas with six of those working for the ministry, I left the department as supervisor of the warehouse. The funny thing was I had to solve many of the problems within the department and find new solutions to old issues no one had ever fixed. In many cases, with the help of the Holy Spirit, I learned how to navigate around some of the people who had caused the problems, otherwise it never would have gotten resolved.

When I first hired on, the boss I had, Mike, looked at me and prophetically said, "I see you have worn your heels off. The road has been difficult, but the Lord will restore those years." I held on to that, and in many ways the Lord has restored much of it and is still restoring it.

My wife also acquired employment with the same ministry, eventually moving up to assistant manager of the kitchen as a Chef. These years were hard, tested many of us in many ways, but we learned many things as we bonded with new friends. It is often said by people when talking about the shortcomings of a ministry that someone will eventually say, "you know, no ministry is perfect!"

It has become like a cliche that people toss out as if that is all the excuse needed to justify the poor actions within the walls of the church. And to some degree they are correct. No ministry is perfect, but all ministries should be moving towards finding the flaws, correcting them, and holding themselves personally to a better standard.

For most of those same people who make these comments, their experience level with ministries is often limited to smaller congregations of a few hundred or less. When a ministry ventures into the larger realms and gains an international presence it becomes a completely different entity. And at no point should Biblical standards be relaxed or justified by bizarre doctrine or actions. In fact, Biblical standards should be held all the more closely. After several bad events, warning dreams, and running into others working in the ministries that shared similar concerns. The Lord was teaching me what was "under the rug", and I was seeing elements of my old dreams come true. These were things no ministry should ever allow, let alone condone, or create "prophetic words" to justify getting around Biblical standards for.

After fifteen years of being in the Fellowship of Ministries with close to six of that on staff, my wife and I turned in our membership. With a song from Ledger called "Foreigner" ringing like a bell in my head, we put the key in the ignition of our truck and drove West. Behind us we left a collection of really good friends, good southern culture, and awesome food.

But the Lord was pointing us back westward. One thing I quickly realized was that I was going to need to do something drastic. I knew I needed to "hit the reset button" on my spiritual thinking. All I really knew was that I was extremely tired of 'church'. I just desperately wanted *Life*. And as the Apostle Paul once said, I now consider it all lost.

As time marched on after leaving the East Coast, the Holy Spirit slowly worked on my thinking. And as with these kinds of things, I eventually started to gain a bit of clarity about the past as the Holy Spirit did his work. Then in the winter of 2019 I got a private message from a ministry in Arizona. It was a prophetic message from Patricia King. I read it and quickly considered it a false prophetic word, so I ignored it and moved on. After a few more months, the Holy Spirit spoke to me that I needed to go back and reread her words to me. It read,

"As I was praying, God opened my eyes to see things around you. There was a certain time when a man of God prophesied in your life and you rejected the instructions of God. This time around you will do as I have said. Believe and you shall obtain total restoration.

I see favor from God. The enemies are working on holding your favor from God. You need to bind it by fasting and prayers, you have not been so devoted in prayers but this time you need enforcement."

As soon as I read this, I suddenly realized the Lord was talking about Dwight and what the Lord was trying to teach me through him. Realizing this was God and that I had rejected this moment of Grace so many years before, I turned around and started doing what I was told.

Since that time the Holy Spirit has accelerated my education and I find myself becoming a little more bold. Willing to say NO more often to the non-Biblical things and say YES to the Biblical. Dreams are starting to increase again and I now see 'whispers' of the things I once knew and walked in so long ago. In fact, it was due to the dreams from the Lord that encouraged me to start writing this book.

Looking Forward.

In giving you an overview I have skipped over a lot of events both high and low to deliver this small snapshot to you. But though it, hopefully you get the idea of some of my journey of the last thirty plus years. So what happened to My Father's House? And why is this book given the title to a church plant that no longer exists?

On the second church plant, when things went to a very low point, I asked the Lord, *what do I do*? I was given a Spiritual encounter for an answer. In that encounter an elderly prophet who died years after this encounter happened, arrived in this dream. In the dream, he walked up to me with the reigns of a brown horse in his hands. Bob Jones had an extremely serious look on his face, he took his index finger and shoved it, painfully into my chest three times. Each time he said the same thing. "My Father's House, the Lord will build it!"

From that encounter I knew it was no longer in my hands. I also knew that when something breaks, the

Lord will build it back stronger than before. Is what the Lord is building just another church plant? Is it a network of churches like some American fast food chain, copied by so many churches in this modern age have become? No, because the Lord will build it, therefore it will not look like anything known of before.

Also, what is coming to the body is beyond the concepts of the *"Seven mountain mandate"* or any of the other concepts being floated around in this age. In fact, it is simpler.

The Wind is Changing.

The Holy Spirit is stirring the body. In some ways, many of us are now becoming restless 'waters', unsettled with the trapping of an artificial reality enclosed in a building, with a glossy web page of smiling faces, polished budget and a mission statement that no one ever reads. We often find ourselves anxious for something we can not describe, but looking around we cannot see it. Impatient, we read of the whispers of another life, illustrated in the lives of Jesus and his Apostles.

So we wait, and wait some more, as we comply with the narrative that we need another bible study, another impartation, another prophetic word, more prayer, another spiritual whatever before we can move forward. In effect, we become subliminally trained to be **"always learning and never able to come to the knowledge of the truth." (2 Timothy 3:7 NASB).** Much of modern Christianity is designed to psychologically manipulate the assembly toward giving to the corporate institution with tax deductions and well-played worship music, heartfelt blessings and misplaced spiritual duty. So that the system of pointless religious repetition stays well-fed and a little more devoid of the life Jesus came to give us everyday.

This manipulation is often highly decorated with the 'things' of church, but not the life of the Lord. Sunday morning follows the same, often predictable, format of music, offering, and preaching. This week looked like the last and that one will look a lot like any given Sunday morning ten years from now. You come in, someone either applies layers of guilt or floods the floor with warm fuzzy words to make you 'feel' good about yourself and the church you are sitting in. Seldom does real education or equipping take place. And if it does, demonic spirits are often soon sent in to pull our minds away as they speak through peoples 'good intentions.' What many now seek, has been longed for by many before us, just like Abraham before us. **"...for he was looking for the city which has foundations, whose architect and builder is God." (Hebrews 11:10 NASB)**

As the reset button gets hit in my life, my eyes are opening to see something larger and bigger and simpler than I could ever conceive or imagine. To quote **1 Corinthians 13:9 WET "...for we know in a partial, fragmentary, incomplete way, and we utter divine revelations in the same way."** What I understand is incomplete and is being added to even as I write this. But based on the comments from many others I have interacted with, I believe that others within the Body of Christ might be getting a glimpse of a new life as well.

So, hopefully what I write here can become a catalyst for discussion and pondering within you and among your group of friends. May you take what I have written here, add it to the things you feel the Spirit is telling you, and make your moment of choice. For it is in the grace filled moments of personal interactions with the Lord at the center, that you and your friends will find the smoldering embers of the wonders of another life.

Let's do the Math.

I have spent an enormous amount of hours pondering, looking, reading, praying. As I have looked at archeological records, modern trends, distant cultures, and other assorted things as I ponder the past. And in between the pages of old books and web pages, the

Lord has used them all to challenge my thinking. As I discard many things to the waste bin and hold close to others, the reset button of my thinking gets hit over and over again as a new level of life is found each time, a little deeper and a little more profound, causing me to wonder even more.

And like others before me, I have started to question our "modern Christianity." At this point I should stop and define what I am saying when I say "Modern Christianity". What I mean is that if it currently exists today then I am talking about it. Charismatic or Non-Charismatic, Baptist or Lutheran, it all carries the same issues at the core.

All I can say for certain is that something was lost, something precious and so simple even a child could understand it. And in some ways it's kind of like C.S. Lewis qualifications for seeing the wonders of Narnia, good for children's eyes but lost on the adults. I believe that what has happened is that we have been culturally trained to trip over it with the traditions of men that have been carefully, skillfully laid down by an Anti-Christ spirit within our walls, so hidden that we often do not even know it exists.

Consider the following, Jesus said;
"You will know them by their fruits. Grapes are not gathered from thorn bushes nor figs from thistles, are they? So every good tree bears good fruit, but the bad tree bears bad fruit. A good tree cannot produce bad fruit, nor can a bad tree produce good fruit. Every tree that does not bear good fruit is cut down and thrown into the fire. So then, you will know them by their fruits." (Matthew 7:16-20 NASB).

Here is a strong biblical principle that can be used for evaluating not only people but movements, churches and teachings. If your teaching produces weak fruit or no fruit at all, then something is wrong at the core and should be corrected.

The experts who have taken a look at church history

have noted that by percentage, the Body of Christ grew the fastest during the first one hundred years. After that came the second and then the third centuries. They were strong, but not as strong as the first. Then, starting in the fourth century things started to seriously derail, slowing the entire body down.

The math of this evaluation is based on current population increase. Nowadays we have big revivals in some countries, but the percentage is low. If the percentage was the same as the Book of Acts, the entire earth would most likely be converted within a lifetime.

Case in point, in the Book of Acts we assume there were around 120 Christians and then the Holy Spirit brought in 3000, that is well over a 2000 percent increase.

Current estimates place the Christian population at around 2.7 Billion. If the Holy Spirit fell on one million people today and they became Christians, that would only be a 0.037 percent increase.

Comparing this information in light of Jesus's teaching on fruit means that something at the core of the Body of Christ is not right and should be corrected. Like the old children's story of the Emperor's new clothes, we are operating under an illusion of what we think we have, and not reality. The Body of Christ has become like what Jesus said to the Assembly of Laodicea.

"You say, 'I am rich; I have acquired wealth and do not need a thing.' But you do not realize that you are wretched, pitiful, poor, blind and naked." (Revelation 3:17 NASB).

"Because you are saying, I am wealthy [in the world's goods] and have gotten [spiritual] riches and have need of not even one thing, and because you do not have a clear and absolute knowledge of the fact that, as for you, *you are the wretched one and a object of pity*, and are poverty-stricken and blind and naked..." (Revelation 3:17 WET).

The Voice of the dead.
FlyLeaf, "This Close."
"Had a dream that we were dead,
But we pretended that we still lived.
With no regrets we never bled and
we took everything life could give.
And came up broken, empty handed in the end.
In the hearts of the blind,
Something you'll never find is a vision of light.
With the voice of the dead, I'm screaming,
I don't know who I love anymore."

To have the one billion soul harvest that so many have prophesied within the Charismatic Evangelical world, tells me that a major transition within the Body needs to take place. Because at this point we are not ready and the Lord knows it. In many ways we are living in the reality of the shadow of Jesus' teaching.

"A pupil is not above the teacher. But everyone who has been completely equipped shall be as his teacher." (Luke 6:40 WET)

The last two thousand years have been marked by a series of disintegrations followed by restoration only to repeat again. And in many ways as each cycle passes, things are lost in the well-intentioned push forward to restore some element of the Body. Teaching and concepts are sometimes lost or watered down under the tyranny of the status quo as it becomes the new normal in the body.

Each student only gets to learn what the teacher can give. And as things fall to the side, each generation not only learns less, but a hidden arrogance slips in making us think we have "learned it all," as we hand out degrees in Theology. We have taught the form, but failed to deliver the life.

We can no longer afford to just press on and restore one part of the Body and assume the other parts are secure. All parts must be raised up together, but this requires a level of integrity, personal commitment, and zeal that few seem to possess.

After thirty plus years of watching things come and go in the church, I often find myself thinking over some of the comments of those far older than myself back in the 80's, as well as events of the past. In the 80's when I encountered the Holy Spirit at my first Vineyard meeting, most of the healings, prophetic words, signs and wonders and casting out of demons were being done by the average normal person. They were abundant and obvious.

As time slowly progressed it seemed to me that the average person was doing less and less as the focus shifted to leadership. Then at some point, to even hear about these kinds of spiritual things happening seemed rare. They were always being done 'some place else'.

Nowadays it seems to me that it is extremely rare that the average person or pastor moves in gifts of power at all. Special meetings with distant speakers are often employed at conferences that are designed just to 'teach' us how to walk in power.

Odd isn't it, the more teaching we obtain in walking in power, the less and less people walk in it?

On the flip side, consider Jesus. He demonstrated it and then told his disciples to go and do it. It was only after they returned that he gave them any teaching at all on healing at all. Do we have things backwards?

Years ago I was asked what I thought about a certain worship service on the East Coast. Everybody was excited about it, my reaction was it was 'ok.' Most blew me off, assuming I did not understand worship or that I had never really experienced 'real' worship.

In my years as a Christian I have most likely attended a few hundred or maybe even a thousand Sunday morning worship services. I can count on one hand all the most notable, two were Vineyard, the third was led by a Native American and the fourth was in the South. In that southern meeting, the entire room could tell the Holy Spirit was moving in power that night, but the pastor rushed to the podium to shut it down for fear it was going to cut into his sermon time. In many ways, the Body has become more and more self-centered, consumed with doctrine and form. And all the things the elderly Christians of my early years warned us about, have become the new normal within western culture and the church. Things no one would have believed in the 1980's are now happening and are accepted, even within the church! Homosexual marriage, legalized drugs, openly mixing the teaching of Christ with other religions. Like a slow motion train wreck played out before us, the church crumbles at the feet of either legalism or lawlessness as people are trained to become powerless.

The Jezebel & Kundalini spirits seem to now run unchecked within much of the church, especially the Charismatic and sadly, few leaders stand up to it, let alone even acknowledge its existence. It bothers me... a lot, that the Spirit of Discernment is nowhere to be found within our walls as a hidden pride of 'what we have become' grows.

We, the Body of Christ, really have become, like it says in the Wuest Expanded Translation, *"...**as for you,** you are the wretched one and a object of pity,..."* **(Revelation 3:17)**

I once attended a church of a 'high' reputation. Few knew that before some of the big conferences that some of the top leaders were in the back with whisky and drugs. High on other 'spirits' a leader would often come out after the worship service and yell to the assembled crowd, "can't you just feel the spirit moving!" To which the crowd would yell and clap in celebration believing he was 'under the anointing.'

It's sad if you think about it. People... the Lords children came from all over. Read the speakers' bios, took time off work, used vacation time, poured money into plane tickets and gasoline pumps. Paid for hotels, got someone to watch their dog at home, all for the 'hope' of a spiritual experience that they have been hungering for. All to be fed a thin meal, devoid of real life changing substance all because the Shepherds are becoming blind and entertaining other spirits.

I would think the Father's children deserve better?

"Many people ministering in meetings give great examples of how to take the spotlight off the Holy Spirit and onto themselves." ~ John Wimber

My Father's House.
Chapter Two
The Pernicious plan

As I have already mentioned, the Spiritual momentum of the Body of Christ is slowing down. I am often reminded of something that was passed around the church thirty years ago. It was a joke, but at the same time serious.

How to ride a Dead Horse

The tribal wisdom of the Dakota Indians, passed on from generation to generation, says that when you discover that you are riding a dead horse, the best strategy is to dismount.

In modern Church Ministries however, a whole range of far more advanced strategies are often employed, such as:

1. Buying a stronger whip.
2. Change riders.
3. Threatening the horse with termination.
4. Appointing a committee to study the horse.
5. Visiting other churches to see how others ride dead horses.
6. Lowering the standards so that dead horses can be included.
7. Re-classifying the dead horse as "living impaired."
8. Hiring outside contractors to ride the dead horse.
9. Harnessing several dead horses together to increase the speed.
10. Attempting to mount multiple dead horses in hopes that one of them will spring to life.
11. Providing additional funding and/or training to increase the dead horse's performance.
12. Doing a productivity study to see if lighter riders would improve the dead horse's performance.
13. Declaring that since the dead horse does not need to be fed, it therefore is less costly, carries lower overhead, and therefore contributes substantially more to the bottom line of the economy of the ministry than do some other horses.
14. Re-writing the expected performance requirements

for all horses.
15. Promoting the dead horse to a supervisory position.

For anyone who has been in a church for any real length of time, we can all smirk together as you and I have most likely seen some of these tactics at one point or another take place within ministry. But, the reality is the fruit of a dead horse ministry will never bring forth life.

Most things I have wandered across in my searching for answers always seem to start with the first century. Various writers and historians examine various aspects of it and then quickly move on to Martin Luther in the Reformation, as if that was the pinnacle of everything 'Christian.' Yes, Luther did many things, but if he had fully restored the body, then I dare say the percentage of new Christians coming in would be of a higher degree than it is today.

I prefer to take a different approach and will include some physical and spiritual history, both good and bad not often examined.

A Bad Tree Grows.

The seeds of this chaos started way back, after the creation of man. The devil did not like what happened, he watched God extending his favor to his new creation and the devil hated every bit of it. To begin to fully understand the disorder of this present age, we need to become aware of a few spiritual realities that are lacking in our current education these days.

In this present age, many churches often totally ignore the spiritual reality of spiritual warfare or pay it very little lip service, belittling the demonic like some badly run company.

As if it was being managed by an evil version of Snow White's seven dwarves, with Satan being nothing more than a red, pointy eared old fool walking around trying to see who he can poke with his pitchfork. **"But Michael the archangel, when he disputed with the**

devil and argued about the body of Moses, did not dare pronounce against him a railing judgment, but said, "The Lord rebuke you!" Jude 1:9 NASB

Consider this, Michael is the leader of God's armies in the Book of Revelation; he was wise enough to treat the devil with respect, due to his power. Micheal knew him before he fell and he knows the power the devil can possess. In essence we are talking about a high level fallen angel who is not burdened with time like we are.

We only have a limited amount of time on earth, quite often the majority of us only gain some real measure of wisdom in the later years of our life before it all ends. We see the end coming, pass on what we can and if our hope is in the Lord and the power of his blood, then Eternity is our next stop and the second death passes over us. For those who refuse, a more permanent death awaits with everlasting torment.

The devil and his forces, they KNOW that torment without rest awaits them. But they have all of time to perfect their knowledge. They have watched, examined and discussed every aspect of human existence and often know what you are going to do before you even know it. Where do you think the root of psychology came from? It came from the dark 'masters' who perfected it.

In the early days of the human race, the first one world government existed for a short time under a leader by the name of Nimrod. According to extra biblical sources, this tyrant started out possibly serving God, then after the devil added his flattering words, the people gave Nimrod all the glory.

Taking a spiritual nose dive, Nimrod delved deep into profound levels of darkness, he and one of his sons Mardon, who most likely became the god Marduk, brought forth the 'dark arts' delivering that knowledge to what eventually became the priests and sorceress of Babylon. Many researchers believe that after the death of Nimrod, his wife Semiramis started promoting her dead husband as a god. Eventually assimilating the local beliefs, Nimrod became Baal and his wife

Semiramis became Ishtar. And so arose the pre-shadows of the Anti Christ spirit.

Centuries passed, wars were fought and eventually Babylon declined in power and with it, the influence of the Babylonian priests was reduced. In 539 BC, Cyrus the great conquered Babylon and the priesthood of Babylon fled the city, traveling west. At some point after 539 they arrived in Pergamum.

"And to the messenger of the assembly in Pergamos write at once: These things says He who has the sharp, two-edged sword. I know with absolute clearness where you settled down and have your dwelling place: where the throne of Satan is located. Yet you are holding fast my Name and did not deny your faith in me even in the days of Antipas, my witness, my faithful one, who was murdered among you, where Satan settled down and has his dwelling place." (Rev 2:12-13 WET).

The Babylonian priests erected the great Acropolis temples of Pergamum in honor of the Greek Pantheon while they also continued to serve the Babylonian god of mystery under the name of Saturnus. The Babylonian mysteries of Nimrod's 'dark arts' were believed to be preserved in the temple of Zeus at Pergamum during these days.

King Attalus III of Pergamon transferred his kingdom into the hands of Rome upon his death in 133 BC. That same year, the Babylonian priests transferred their dark teachings to Rome. With them they brought many gods and goddesses including Mithra, Tammuz and Cybele who wore the fish mitre on her head that is so often seen on today's popes.

These events happened during the time when Tiberius Gracchus was trying to bring about land reforms in the Empire, to transfer land back into the hands of the common citizens to stabilize the Empire. This act, if followed, would have given the people not only their land back, but would have taken away a measure of power from the elites of the Empire.

Tiberius Gracchus was assassinated shortly thereafter and a Roman civil war soon broke out. The penetration of the religion of Babylon into Rome became so invasive that Rome was for a time called "The New Babylon".

For some 630 years after 539 BC, the Babylonian priests lived and expanded their influence in the Empire by assimilating the local Greek/Roman godhead system into their own. Their power in Pergamum was so effective that Jesus declares that Pergamum was Satan's very home.

On a modern historical side note, on September 9th, 1878 archeologists unearthed Satan's throne in Pergamum and moved it to Berlin, Germany. Albert Speer, the great Nazi architect, studied and used this throne to build a giant replica of it for Adolph Hitler. This replica, called the *Zeppelintribüne* became Hitler's  pulpit from which he released the greatest horrors of World War Two. After the war, the Soviet Leader Kruschev took it to Leningrad in 1948. But the original throne was soon returned to Berlin, apparently all the paranormal activity around Satan's throne spooked Kruschev.

Nowadays the throne sits in a museum named the "Pergamum Museum." So yes, despite the flawed teaching of some church denominations, Satan still carries a lot of power.

In the Bible I now use a lot, *Wuest Expanded Translation*, I find it interesting Jesus's description of the devil in **John 17:16.** Jesus calls him, **"the pernicious one"**. The definition of pernicious is a great description of the devil's tactics. Pernicious is defined as: "Having a harmful effect, especially in a gradual or subtle way." That means Satan's influence is rarely sudden, but is often well planned out. Paul also said, **"so that no advantage would be taken of us by Satan, for we are not ignorant of his schemes." (2 Corinthians 2:11 NASB).**

Out of this one reality, two things become clear to me. One is that the Lord of Heaven and Earth wants us to be fully aware of how the devil works. Second is that by the fruit of this present church age... we are highly unaware of *how* the devil works.

But let's return to the historical timeline.

From the base in Pergamum, the Babylonian/Roman priests expanded their influence deep into Rome itself, most likely becoming the main force behind the Christian persecutions. Rome, for centuries, had adapted the local religions by assimilation, creating many blurred lines between each other's gods. And in time all of them started looking very similar.

Zeus and Jupiter, for example, after some time started looking a lot like each other, just with different names.

How much Rome's policy of cultural assimilation was influenced by the Babylonian priests is unclear but it is obvious it did happen. In time, many nasty Caesars rose up in an attempt to destroy the Christians. One by one they all in time fell away as the Empire made political alliances trying to hold their shaky empire together. Centuries of war, betrayal, and deception was taking its toll, making it increasingly harder and harder for the Roman Senate to preserve the Empire.

During these early centuries the Body of Christ had spread out over many thousands of miles. Deep into Africa, India and all the way into the British Isles. Many of these communities of faith held close to what they knew from the Apostles' teachings. And by the evidence of their rapid spread, The New Babylon, Rome was realizing the issue of the Christians containment was now far beyond what they could control.

Rome had tried, many times, to crush the leadership of the Body by killing off the senior "bishops" only to find that another one would simply stand up and take the place of the first.

And even though Jerusalem had suffered many attacks, famines, and burnings, historians now know that there was an unbroken line of Apostolic bishops in Jerusalem with the Apostle John as the first Bishop, as mentioned in the Book of Acts. With a measure of influence over the whole body, this line of leaders maintained the historical Apostolic gospel of the Kingdom.

Much of that took a major detour in the year 312 AD. Emperor Constantine of Rome had a conversion to Christ. This quickly led to the legalization of Christianity throughout the empire. Although many welcomed the ending to the persecution, there were still many who realized this could allow profound problems to enter into the Body.

The rules of life had changed for Christians. Before this, you were either completely in, forsaking everything to follow Christ or you were not. After the legalization, a person did not need to be fully in. Lukewarmness, complacency and toleration that was always present, now had better soil to grow in.

Was Constantine's conversion to Christ real? We may never know this side of Eternity, but it is obvious to me that several historians feel his conversion was politically motivated in an effort to save Rome by assimilating the stronger religion.

Many good things did take place as a result of his conversion, like assembling the Bible we have today. And with a simple search on the internet a person can easily find a long list of his 'better' qualities that many Catholic sites report. But if we look at the fruit of history after 312 AD we find many problems rose up, causing serious problems in the household of faith.

One of the problems we have in the church is the exultation of man. This is a common problem in every church today. We raise up a leader, often the Pastor, to unrealistic levels. And in many ways we are like the Israelites of old who turned Saul into a king over Israel. We take men, promote them, tossing the glory that is reserved for God on them. This makes men spiritually unstable, because Man was never made to be worshiped. This I feel is most likely one of the hidden causes of Pastor burnout. It's easy to say, "stop worshiping the pastor", but in reality I think the way our modern Christianity is designed is the bigger problem.

But what else happened?

It is often said that history is written by the victors. In truth, it is written by those who control the flow of money and power. Today many historical Christian communities have been slowly painted over with the broad brush of Catholicism, giving us a weaker view of our own history. I am grateful for the few who have put their foot down and said no to the revisions as well as some of the old books that still exist like *Foxe's Book of Martyrs* that comes to us from the sixteenth century.

Constantine was quickly accepted as the "Man of God," and as a result, the historical line of Jewish Apostolic bishops in Jerusalem came to an end as everyone shifted away from them to Constantine as the new leader. On a larger scale, we as the Body of Christ have done this with various political leaders over the years. We did it with Charlemagne, and in many ways we are doing it with Donald Trump even now.

In 323 AD Pope Sylvester the First, moved the Sabbath day from Saturday to Sunday. He named it "the Lord's day" and commanded by law that everyone should keep it. The hidden meaning behind this was not lost on the former Roman citizens who had accepted Christ. This is because it was well known in the empire that the sun god Mithra had one day a week dedicated solely to him, Sunday. And as the 'lord' of the sun this day was considered the "lord's day" long before 323 AD.

In 345 AD Pope Julius the First, officially set the date of December 25 for the celebration of the Nativity or Christmas.

Note: this is seen by many, including myself, as an assimilation tactic. As the original Jewish Christian bishops were becoming ignored, the popularity of declaring Peter as the head church was promoted and the names of many others in history were soon included to add legitimacy to the claim of an unbroken line of popes. Thereby creating a historical narrative that Catholicism was always "the real church".

Also during these early days, the Roman Catholics raised up many buildings and placed within them statues of the twelve apostles. This was seen as an offensive to many true believers who held to the understanding **"You shall not make for yourself an idol, or any likeness of what is in heaven above or on the earth beneath or in the water under the earth" (Exodus 12:4 NASB).**

This became a growing concern that is still shared by many today that the images of the "saints" were nothing more than the recycled images of the old Roman gods renamed. Jupiter became Peter, Mercury became Philip and Cupid became John.

Moment by moment, day by day, the old standards of Christianity got reinvented, assimilated, and turned into a political powerhouse for the elites of Rome. Missionaries got relabeled as Monks and terms like Cardinal soon entered the vocabulary. As Jesus' mother,

Mary soon got remade into the image of the "Queen of Heaven" **(Jeremiah 7:18)** with the qualities of Juno, Ishtar, Cybele and Hera all blended together for the 'faithful' of the church to adore within Mary.

The symbolism of this was also not lost on the early Christians of that day, as it could be easily seen as it is today in Rome a statue of Mary throwing a thunderbolt like the goddess Athena.

The once simple understanding that Jesus was the only door you needed to the Father was soon supplanted by Mary and a long list of "patron saints" to pray to in the hopes 'they' would speak on your behalf.

The growing uneasiness felt by many Christians of that day guided them to seek refuge in various corners of the Empire. Time passed and the illusion of religious freedom quickly evaporated as the persecution of the Body of Christ continued and intensified.

What the old Roman Empire did in persecutions under the Caesars never fully stopped, and in many places in the new *'Holy'* Roman Empire became marked with layers of bloodshed. In effect, the Caesars became Popes and the death toll increased in larger numbers as the authority of the Popes advanced over the land like oil on water.

Your options as a believer in Christ were you could either join the 'church' and bow to the authority of the pope so that you could live freely in life. Or you could learn to hide in order to stay true to the convictions you were taught in secret communities scattered around the known world.

Trembling with concern, the Body of Christ moved out and away from Catholic dominated lands. Families abandoned their homes and took refuge in the hills and mountains of Europe.

By the start of the fourth century, many of the Christians in Southern Europe were becoming known as the "Insabbati". *The people of the sabbath.* Protests grew into a spiritual rebellion against the introduction of pagan practices into Christianity by the Catholics who the Christians referred to as 'The New Comers.' In time these communities that were scattering to the wilderness became known by other names like Leonists, Vallenses, Vaudois and Valsenses from which eventually became known as the Waldenses.

The Waldensians became known as the "people of the valleys". In these places they continued to maintain a deep apostolic faith that they traced down from the original twelve apostles. Meeting in mountain caves to worship, teach, or hide from the pope's soldiers, their communities built a tenacity to hang on that lasted for hundreds of years. Many were captured and thrown from the mountain cliffs or in one case, eighty of them were collected to be all burned alive together.

Rise of the Celts

In the fifth century a man who would later become known as the 'Apostle of Ireland' started converting Ireland. Patrick became known for some of his signs and wonders as well as the community that was built.

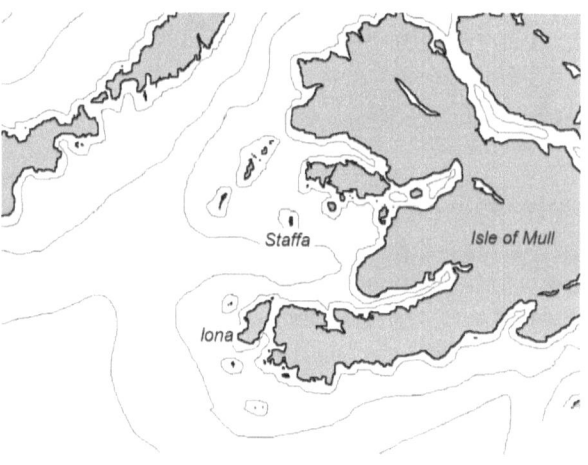

Please note, I am refusing to use the term 'saint' with his name. Because according to the Bible we who are called into Christ are all saints. The term saint, due to Catholic influence has become a 'mark of special distinction', often elevating the person to a place of worship. The reality is Patrick was an Apostolic Missionary, confirmed with signs and wonders, and he gave rise to what we now refer to as Celtic Christianity.

The example Patrick provided for his followers continued as a generation later another Celtic Christian by the name of Colm Cille, also known as Columba, was raised up. He left Durry, Ireland in 563 AD with two hundred followers to the Scottish Island of Iona. These were not 'Monks' and they did not build monasteries as some now believe. Patrick, Columba, and the others who followed were missionaries who built educational training centers. Iona, in time, became one of the highest quality schools in Europe excelling in Biblical studies and science.

These students lived, sang, and laughed in the healthy Christian community of Iona. Learning to bake, tend farm animals, cultivate crops, prayer and fasting. They held close to the tradition of commandments as the Apostles taught. And this lighthouse of the Lord continued for 641 years until the Catholic Benedictine monks drove them out.

In 596 AD, Pope Gregory I sent Augustine of Canterbury to bring the English under catholic submission. In 601 AD Augustine traveled to the Welsh countryside and met with a student of Columba by the name of Dnooth, also known as Dunod, and the Celtic Welsh community he had formed in Bangor-on-dee.

Augustine ordered them all to convert to Catholicism. They refused and according to history, Augustine returned with the Saxon army, killing 1200 students. Isn't it interesting that the butcher of Bangor is now considered a "saint."

In 643 AD, King Oswald of Northumbria requested a missionary from Iona be sent to Northumbria to teach the people about Jesus. Iona sent Aidan, and Aidan requested the Island of Lindisfarne to set up his community. Aidan was a man of practical faith and strong personality. He often used the funds he collected to ransom slaves and care for the poor. He also delivered many prophetic words that came true.

The Spiritual Lighthouse of Lindisfarne soon 'exploded' across what we now know as the British Isles. Finnis succeeded Aidan and Colman succeeded Finnis. And in a few short years, centuries of Paganism was nearly driven away at a rapid pace off the islands to be replaced with Celtic Christianity.

Unfortunately an event would arrive that would cause a major problem. A man by the name of Wilfred was studying in Rome during the time of Pope Vitalian. He was fully intent on bringing the "Celtic Church into *submission* under the authority of Rome."

Catholicism had a small influence on the island during those days. King Oswy of Bernicia, whose brother was most likely King Oswald, became the 'judge' over the spiritual debate. The leaders of the Celtic Church, Hilda and Colman were invited to attend the debate with Wilfred to settle the 'proper' date for Easter. Wilfred had been studying for this argument for three years and he was completely drilled in all the papal arguments. Colman had only been in charge for a few years before the Synod of Whitby in the kingdom of Bernicia was called.

On one hand was Colman and on the other was Wilfred and King Oswy's wife, Eanflæd, who was a catholic. Colman skillfully kept up his end and was slowly winning the debate on the issue of Easter before the King, when Wilfred changed his tactics. Using the argument of Peter's authority over the church, Wilfred convinced the King that by extension of the right of succession of authority, that Colman's argument had to be wrong because only catholic authority was correct.

King Oswy was convinced and (by law) the people of Whitby were ordered to convert to Catholicism. Colman and many of the Celtic Church then retreated north and eventually back to Iona. Hilda however elected to stay in Bernicia. In slightly over a hundred years, the Celtic Lighthouse of Lindisfarne was attacked by the first Viking raids on the British Isles. As the light failed, the darkness of paganism rolled over the Island once more, reasserting its ancient hand.

The Roman Catholic policy of 'evangelizing' the people by means of the sword, law of the land or political alliances only continued to display to the people the obvious differences between Christ and the antiChrist system that was strangling Europe.

The Wind across Europe changes.

In January of 1198, a new stronger power rose up in Rome, and with that power not only did the evil wind extend its hand, but a spiritual earthquake started to push back against the devil's grip. Pope Innocent the Third rose to power, bent on bringing everything from Ireland to Jerusalem under Catholic domination.

As evidenced by the fact that the crusaders took Constantinople the same year the order was given for the monks to take the last Celtic lighthouses in 1204.

In England, King John and the Pope got into an ongoing feud in 1208 over issues within England. The next year, deep in southern France the Albigensian community had a dark wind rise up. France had become their home as they spread out, over taking many of the cities with their communities. However, in 1209, Pope Innocent the Third, out of demonic zeal, decided that groups like this should be exterminated in order to 'save the church'. Pulling together an army, Pope Innocent, who was not innocent, waged a twenty year 'holy war' against the real saints.

Trading promises of salvation for murder, the army flooded France at the beginning of the war, bringing destruction and death to the land. Seeing what was happening, the Albigensians ran for the safety of the walled city of Béziers. Unfortunately many of the pope's army made it in before the gates were closed.

According to reports, the city streets ran red with blood and no one including the youngest children were spared. Screaming, "Kill all, kill all!" the massacre continued without stopping until the city was lit on fire, burning it to the ground. Historians debate the number of the dead, from as low as 20,000 and upwards to 60,000 Christians were killed and soon the army turned from the destroyed city to do the same to the surrounding villages killing even more. The Albigensian campaign, as it became known, lasted for twenty years, hunting them down in every place the army could find them.

The War for a Home

With the passing of the first thousand years, changes had started to grow. Small at first but persistent as the seeds laid down by the hidden Waldensian and Celtic communities in the corners of Europe grew and the Holy Spirit used them to start laying a foundation for later generations to work with.

For centuries the Waldensians had withstood one attack after another in the secluded valleys of Europe. But unfortunately in the 12th and 13th centuries, compromise had started to find inroads into the Waldensian communities. The Waldensians pretended to live as Roman Catholics, attending the Holy Mass and having their children baptized in Catholic churches to "keep up the image" of being a good Catholic. Privately however they stuck to their beliefs behind closed doors.

Compromise, however, never works out for believers, as spiritually you are telling the demonic realm that you have given in and accepted their orders. And once you decide to turn away from the compromise, into the light, a demonic rage begins to build, seeking retribution for your turning away from them.

The demonic started to feel its grasp loosen in 16th century Europe, with the first publication of several Bibles, and then the rise of Martin Luther. As the Reformation spread across the land, whispers of this new wind reached the valleys of Italy and the Waldensians sent people to ask for more information.

In 1532 the Waldensian called everyone to gather for the Synod of Chanforan, to speak with the reformers. This lit a new fire in the Waldensians Community causing them to start openly declaring their beliefs as Waldensian before the people around them.

In the Celtic lands of the North, the Protestant Reformation strongly took hold. While it became a political tool of the British crown, it sank deep into the hearts of the people of Scotland.

King Henry the Eighth of England whose rebellion

against Rome and turning toward his own self-serving version of Protestantism died in 1547 leaving his nine year old son Edward as the new King. Edward quickly encouraged it to grow and Protestantism took a serious leap forward.

Unfortunately Edward was never really a healthy person. And in 1553 his health took a serious turn for the worse. At some point, an unknown woman visited and started treating him for his illness against the doctors' orders. Edward's limbs quickly swelled and his hair and nails fell out. The woman quickly disappeared leaving everyone to suspect poison.

Seeing the end, Edward named Lady Jane Gray to replace him so that the Catholics will not return to power. Jane Gray unfortunately was Queen for only nine days when Edwards' sister Mary, who had already raised a Catholic army, took the throne and killed Jane Gray and her husband.

To the north the newly established protestant congregations of Presbyterians established and signed the First Covenant of Scotland at Edinburgh in 1557. In totally defiance to the demonic rule of Europe and submission to Jesus they created the first mass covenant as a nation between themselves and God. Here is an excerpt that displays the attitude present in the Covenant.

"WE perceiving how Satan in his members, the Antichrists of our time, cruelly do rage, seeking to overthrow and destroy the Gospel of Christ, and his Congregation, ought, according to our bounden duty, to strive in our Master's Cause, even unto the death, being certain of the Victory in him..."

This zeal **(John 2:17)** was so strong that mass meetings throughout the nation were common and the Queen of England "Bloody Mary" who had killed many of her own people for being protestant, shut herself up behind armed guards for fear of an uprising. By this time, the crown of England had flipped back to Catholic and a former bodyguard of an earlier preacher who carried a big sword by the name of John Knox was rising to the head of the Scottish nation as the new spiritual leader.

Three years later in 1560, the Scottish Parliament abolished all Catholic authority in the nation and then adopted the Reformed Scots Confession of Faith.

These are not isolated incidents. Between the 1500's and the 1600's thousands and thousands were killed as they struggled for freedom all across Europe and even America. This push for freedom, in my opinion, caused a major backlash against them with the massacre of Huguenots in Fort Caroline Florida in 1565.

A Jesuit Priest, Don Pedro Mendez de Aviles, was released from prison for horrific crimes and sent to the new world to subdue the Protestants. Leaving Europe with eleven ships he only had five left after an encounter with a hurricane. It is estimated that around 300 to 400 people were slaughtered by this Jesuit Priest and to this day the place is called Matanzas Inlet, meaning the "bay of slaughter." History, unfortunately, has painted him in a good light and today a statue of him stands before the St. Augustine's city hall.

Within a few short years, a handful of survivors returned to Europe after claiming they trudged their way through the swamps of the south all the way to what is now Texas before finding a ship to take them back.

Then seven years later in 1572 the Catholics unleashed a new massacre in Paris called the St. Bartholomew Day massacre that was truly horrific in scale. It is most likely unknown how many Christians died in the decades of bloodshed this caused. But to help sum up the mental image of it, here is a quote from *Foxe's book of Martyrs* that has several pages dedicated to this event,

Concerning the siege of the City of Rochelle.
"...besieged it seven months; though by their assaults, they did very little executions on the inhabitants, yet by famine, they destroyed eighteen thousand out of two and twenty. The dead, being too numerous for the living to bury, became food for vermin and carnivorous birds."

During this time many Nobles were congratulated and rewarded for their efforts in killing the Protestants.

Also during this year Queen Mary was replaced by a Queen who was more giving towards the Protestants, Elizabeth the First. The Pope, fearing the growth of a Protestant nation in Britain, sent the Spanish Armada in 1588 with 130 ships to invade England. With a much smaller force, that many consider being protected by the hand of God, they not only stopped the invasion but also chased many warships up into the rocky shores, with a total loss of 20,000 Spanish soldiers.

The next year, King Henry the Fourth of France started putting an end to the killing with the Edict of Nantes, granting Protestants a lot of freedom under the law. Henry for years had fought against many of the massacres with his rebel forces until he was named King. This event put him at odds with the "Holy League" who was a collection of influential Roman Catholics in places of power. This League was one of the main forces that encouraged the killing, giving orders to the field commanders.

Unfortunately, Evil never sleeps and it will always keep working to find new roads into places it once held. Queen Elizabeth was soon replaced after this with King James the first whom many historians strongly believe was bi-sexual and a Mason. In fact the author of the King James Bible common nickname in England was Queen James. James son, Charles came to the crown after him, and is considered by many a man of "little backbone". Charles was then beheaded in 1649 for treason by the government of England.

A Puritan Commander-in-Chief, Lord Oliver Cromwell was then put in charge and led the armies of the Parliament of England. Cromwell's rise happened at a crucial time for the Protestants of Europe in 1655.

With over a hundred years of Protestant spread since the Synod of Chanforan, the Duke of Savoy whose grandfather was a Huguenot moved against the Waldensians in 1655. Arriving in the lower valleys in the winter, he gave them a choice, "attend mass or leave the valleys!"

Not willing to comply, the Waldensian moved over two thousand people across frozen rivers and narrow mountain passes to the Waldensian communities higher up in the mountains. The Duke however did not honor his own order and returned in April at four in the morning with an army to deliver a surprise attack. He had promised his army he would nullify their prison sentences if they did this job for him.

I am "taming down" the graphic details that history records. The Dukes army constantly found ways of terrorizing, traumatizing and butchering the people. Babies were tossed over the cliffs or ripped apart. Many families took off to even higher elevations to freeze to death in the snow. Fathers were forced to wear the heads of their children around their necks before being tossed from the cliffs of Mount Castelluzzo themselves. Thousands lay dead in the valley below Castelluzzo as the rest of the valleys were soon littered with the dead in horrific display.

Word of the massacre spread to England who at that

time had its Puritan protector, Lord Oliver Cromwell. Hearing the reports, he called for donations for the refugees and let it be known he was going to send the English Navy if the massacre that was spreading to other places was not stopped.

Fearing a Protestant invasion in Catholic lands, the massacre quickly came to an end. Unfortunately Cromwell's leadership came to an end soon after and England found itself with another Catholic King who was enforcing his rule, just like the others before him, over the land.

In 1685, King Louis the 14th of France replaced the Edict of Nantes with his own creation, the Edict of Fontainebleau. Seeing that the Edict of Nantes had been revoked and the Protestants were starting to die once more, William of Orange raised an army and invaded England in 1688 at Torbay and captured James the 2nd, forcing the Catholics back in England. His mother was Mary, Princess of Orange, the daughter of King Charles I of England, Scotland, and Ireland. His victory made him King of those lands as well and gave the Protestants of Europe a safe land to go to.

The Waldensians fight back

Possibly encouraged by William's pushback, a Waldensian pastor by the name of Henri Arnaud, feeling the call of God a year later in 1689 to retake the homeland, rallied an army. And on his second attempt he led and army of 800 Waldensians back into the valleys to attack a force of 3000 at a mountain bridge. In a spectacular battle, only 15 Waldensian died retaking the bridge, confusion settled into the Catholic army as they started killing each other. By the time the battle for the valley was done, the pastors' small army had resisted and overcome a force of 22,000 in the middle of winter.

Cleaning out their old churches, burning the Catholic idols, Henri Arnaud led his warriors in song as they sang Psalm 74:18-22 together.

"Remember this, Lord, that the enemy has taunted You, And a foolish people has treated Your name disrespectfully. Do not give the soul of Your turtledove to the wild animal; Do not forget the life of Your afflicted forever. Consider the covenant; For the dark places of the land are full of the places of violence. May the oppressed person not return dishonored; May the afflicted and the needy praise Your name." Psalm 74:18-22 NASB

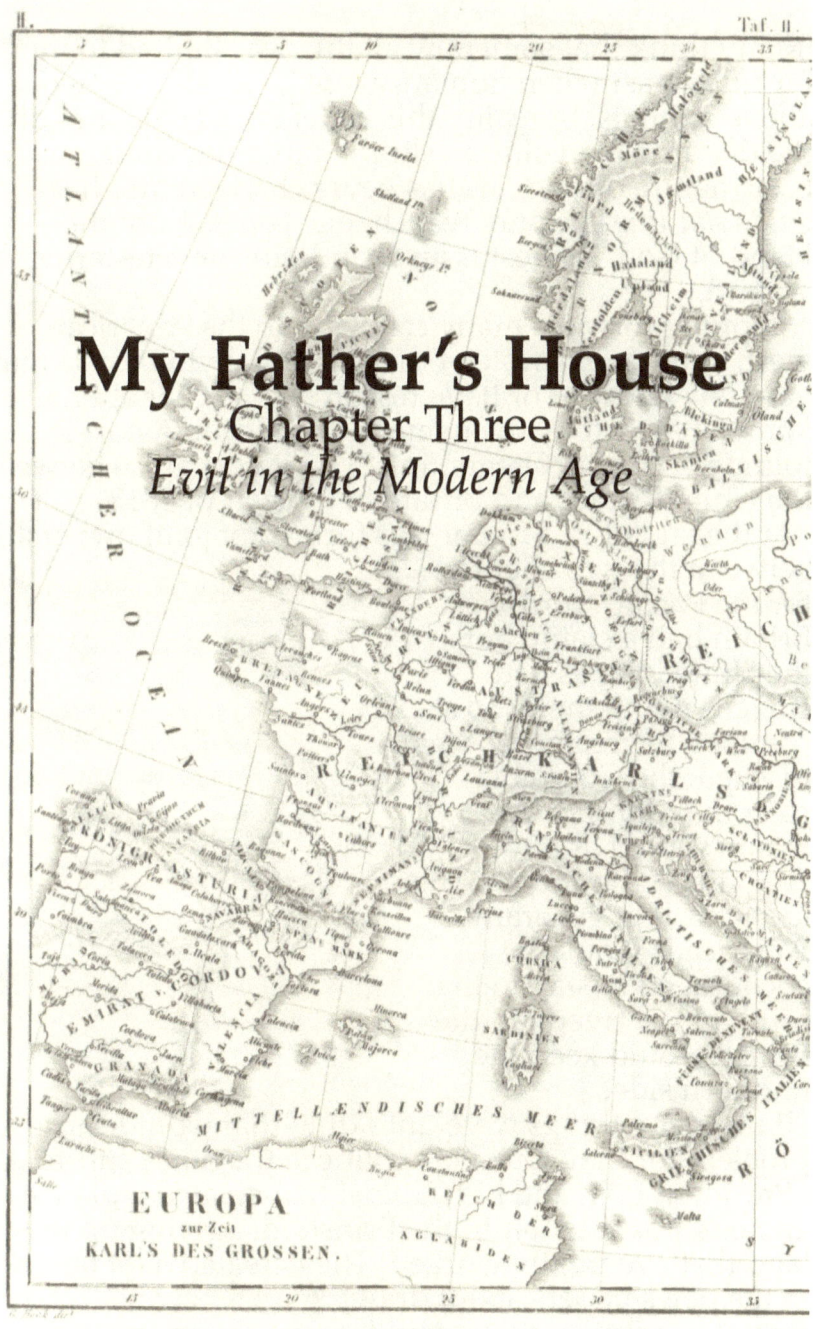

My Father's House
Chapter Three
Evil in the Modern Age

Many think that somehow all this was limited to the far-flung past when humans were just a step or two above animals. In reality this belief is just evidence of the doctrine of evolution slipping into our thinking. The basic nature of humans has never changed, nor has evil's nature. The only real change comes from the Hand of God, the rest is just band-aids on a festering wound.

Stepping forward many centuries to the American west, another example of the evil of Babylon exists that very few know of or have researched. A year after a known Satanist by the name of John Jacob Astor founded Astoria, Oregon in 1811, conflict arose between the United States and Britain in the war of 1812.

At the end of it, a treaty was formed of joint ownership between the two countries for the Pacific Northwest. Britain had a claim, but the United States had citizens living there. So a common "agreement" was reached, the Columbia river that divided the region served as an "unofficial" boundary. The idea was that generally Americans would be encouraged to stay to the south of the river and the British would keep the northern side.

But several things were unfolding that would cause a problem for that. One was political, the other spiritual.

President Polk and his Cabinet had created a plan, a game of poker to 'bluff' the British into giving up the land that eventually worked. They created a lot talking in the news papers about drawing up a new boundary far to the north or they would go to war for the third time with Britain. Their desire was the 49th parallel, so they created the war cry of "54/40 or fight!" That was much further to the north.

This message flooded the papers in both America and Europe. In time, the plan worked, it was brilliant, the British gave in and conceded to having a new boundary drawn up along the 49 parallel. This forced the British to look into other options of maybe getting it back.

Seeing how well the policy of religious separation worked in Ireland, getting the Irish to fight each other, The Hudson Bay company encouraged two Jesuit priests by the name of Blanchet and Deemers to venture out into the west. With the plans to enter the tribal villages and erect a Catholic houses of worship directly across from the Protestant churches.

To add to this, the Lord had raised up a local tribal leader by the name of Spokan Garry. He was the son of a chief, and his father allowed him to be taken away to the Red River mission in Canada for spiritual education.

Returning home, Garry became a powerful voice of evangelism, teaching the young in a school he built about Christ. His work opened the door for the largest west coast revival in tribal America that was never recorded in Christian history books. Thousands came to Christ as his message spread as far north as one hundred mile house in Canada and as far south as the Great Salt Lake.

Soon the sons of other chiefs came to learn and they then spread the work of Jesus around the frontier as names like Kootenay Collins, Cayuse Halket, Spokane Berens, Ellice and Pitt of the Nez Perces were soon added to the roster of Native Christian ministers covering the land.

In Washington Irving's book, *"The Adventures of*

Captain Bonneville,"(1837)

Irving writes about the fruit of the ministry of Ellice and Pit:

"Simply to call these people religious," he says, *"would convey but a faint idea of the deep hue of piety and devotion which pervades their whole conduct. Their honesty is immaculate..."*

Then in another chapter he writes:

"They are certainly more a nation of saints than a horde of savages."

Blanchet and Deemers had an uphill battle before them. Not only were local tribal leaders truly devoted to the true Jesus, but the white Methodist and Presbyterian missionaries had arrived almost ten years before them. Of them, Marcus and Narcissa Whitman now had a training base among the Cayuse people. The Whitmans set up a Christian community complete with orchards, gardens, training school, blacksmith shop, sawmill, gristmill, and a collection of dikes, ditches and ponds for irrigation. Narcissa ran the school with over 200 students while her husband managed the rest.

Unfortunately in time, smallpox entered the area again and so did the Catholic missionaries Blanchet and Deemer with a wooden board they named, "the Catholic ladder." Using it as a teaching aid, the 'ladder' displayed a series of marks on the board. The top marks were, of course, reserved for God and Mary and under them were the marks representing the two priests and marks for everyone else below them. With this they explained Heaven, Hell, Purgatory and their own personal relationship with Heaven.

Undermining the Whitmans work with doubt, fear and a false gospel. Marcus Whitman had enough of their deceptive words. Pulling the board away from the priests' hands, he explained to the Cayuse that the Catholics have always persecuted the Protestants. Smearing the blood of a steer across the face of the priests' ladder, he prophesied that their evil would bring, *"a greater blood that would bathe the Cayuse country.*" This prophecy came to pass a few years later in 1847.

With the unending problem of smallpox and the whispers of the Catholic priests insinuating that the disease came from the 'evil' Whitmans. A boiling point was soon reached and several warriors one day slipped in behind Marcus and Narcissa and killed them.

The Oregon territory soon erupted into war, dividing many tribal and white communities. Although rumors are hard to confirm during a war, many people felt that the root of some of the "Indian wars," between the native people of the territory and the white settlers was at least religiously motivated by the Catholics.

Tribal America

Decades passed and North America continued to progress over the decades. Roads were paved, cities grew, and the Native Americans suffered in silence as Catholics gained political power in the United States and Canada. Many tribal nations like the Métis, Cree, Ojibway, Algonquin in Canada bore the dark weight of the "Indian tribal schools". These forced eugenics programs decimated many tribes as children were beaten and raped into submission. Current estimates of the number of missing native children conservatively sits around 60,000.

Note: I am not going to reprint the testimonies I have read connected to this horrific period of time. Basically, animals were treated better than children.

Like many survivors of horrific events, they lived in silent pain, unaware that the Roman Catholics were fully engaged in this kind of hideous activity in other places in the world.

Spain.

Starting in 1936 Dictator Franco ruled the nation. Under his rule the Catholic Church had unrestricted power to deal with orphans however they wanted. In a long standing history of lying, stealing, and falsifying records, Catholic orphanages constantly lied to single mothers, telling them that their child was stillborn because of their sin. Weighing down these poor single girls with the guilt that they had killed their own child with their sin because God was angry with them.

Today there is a strong movement of thousands of mothers in Spain protesting in the streets, demanding answers.

Children were often sold outright to faraway families and told to burn the original records when they got home. Once they arrived back in their home country, the local priests would often help them to create new birth certificates. Current estimates place the number of stolen children around 300,000. The fight for truth continues to this day.

Ireland.

The Children of Tuam. For 36 years in the early to mid twentieth century, The Bon Secours Sisters ran a "special home" of horrors. In 2012 an amateur historian, Catherine Corless decided to write an essay about the home for a local journal.

Running into roadblocks she started talking to the local people of Tuam. As her eyes started to open, she eventually heard the story of some young boys in the

1970's who climbed the stone wall of the abandoned orphanage to pick apples. The boys jumped from the wall and landed on something in the court yard that sounded hollow. Finding a way to open up the large container below their feet, they discovered the horrific sight of large numbers of skeletons.

What happened? I will not go into the horrific details, but here is a quote from Edna Kenny, former prime minister of Ireland speaking before parliament on this issue (2011 - 2017). *"We took their babies. And we gifted them, or we sold them, or we trafficked them, or we starved them, or we neglected them, or we denied them to the point of their disappearance from our hearts and our sight, from our country. And in the case of Tuam, and possibly other places, from life itself."*

Scotland
Smyllum Park Orphanage run by the Daughters of Charity of St Vincent de Paul. Bodies of 402 orphans found in a mass grave.

United States
Judy Byington of Child Abuse Recovery website reported the following on June 21, 2014:
"As of November 2013, over ten million Catholic Priest child sex abuse cases have been documented. These 10,077,574 cases represented a mere fraction of total crimes committed. Only an estimated 10% of sex abuse victims were thought to speak out about their sexual abuse and just 10% of those cases saw the inside of a courtroom."

In a report from Associated Press dated October 4, 2019. Claudia Lauer and Meghan Hoyer broke a story concerning oversight of known pedophilies. *"Nearly 1,700 priests and other clergy members that the Roman Catholic Church considers credibly accused of child sexual abuse are living under the radar with little to no oversight from religious authorities or law enforcement, decades after the first wave of the church abuse scandal roiled U.S. dioceses, an Associated Press investigation has found."*

"These priests, deacons, monks and lay people now teach middle-school math. They counsel survivors of sexual assault. They work as nurses and volunteer at nonprofits aimed at helping at-risk kids. They live next to playgrounds and daycare centers. They foster and care for children."

"And in their time since leaving the church, dozens have committed crimes, including sexual assault and possessing child pornography, the AP's analysis found."

As you can see, as we examine the fruit of the tree, it's not good. In fact it is evil in its darkest form. Any historical, consistent pattern of an organization like this should not be ignored and just patted on the back as if it was a child who accidentally broke the neighbor's window.

This pattern you have read is only the *smallest example* of what is most likely millions of lives destroyed by the Anti-Christ Babylonian system. But, what about today, what is happening today?

Let's take a look at a 'snapshot' of modern history surrounding a strange set of 'events,' that are spiritual in nature and should make a person ponder the symbolism and message of what is being said. Let's start with Pope Benedict.

• Jan 28, 2013, Pope Benedict with the help of children released a dove out the window. The dove is attacked by a seagull. The pope looks disturbed.
• Feb 11, 2013, Fifteen days later, Pope Benedict announces his resignation, shortly thereafter (a few hours) two bolts of lightning strike the dome of St. Peter's basilica.

- March 13, 2013, per tradition, the world awaits the election of the new Pope.
  Using an old chimney and smoke system to notify the world by the color of the smoke. The world watches as a seagull lands on top of the chimney and sits until the smoke arrives. Jorge Mario Bergoglio, a cardinal with a shadowy past, mired in the ongoing questions of the disappearance of hundreds of Children from Argentina is elected, taking up the name, "Frances."
- Jan 19, 2014, Pope Francis delivers a message from his window on the Lamb of God, encouraging grace, forgiveness and starts laying the foundation for 'inclusiveness.' Five hours later on his home continent of South America the statue of 'Christ the Redeemer is struck by lighting, seriously damaging the right hand.
- Jan 26, 2014, Pope Francis with the help of children releases a pair of doves from his window. One is attacked by a seagull, the other by a crow. Francis does not look pleased.
- Feb 11, 2014, one year to the day of Benedict's resignation. A six foot bronze statue of the Greek god Apollo is discovered in Gaza. Some historians refer to his followers as a Eugenics cult, because this "Hyperborean" invader from the north was viewed as the perfect embodiment of all the gods. And that his body perfection should be followed by everyone, even to the point of removing the "undesired." The statue was estimated to be 2000 years old and quickly disappeared without a trace.
- April 14, 2014, the Passover week of the 14th to 22nd begins at the same time as the blood moon.
- On the 20th. Easter mass in Rome, the following message is declared to the crowd in a song. "*His flame, Lucifer, drawing his own creation. Man, I say, O Lucifer, who knows no setting. Christ your Son who came back from the dead, and shed his peaceful light to the human race, is alive and reigns forever and ever!*" {**yes, in case you're wondering, you did read this quote correctly, the pope is declaring Jesus to be the son of Lucifer**}

- On the 22nd. A statue of the goddess Mary falls over to strike a priest on the head during the Easter parade in Spain.
- On the 25th. A statue of Christ on the cross falls over, killing a man just ahead of Pope Frances motorcade.
- May 23, 2014, Pope Francis arrives in the Holy Land and lightning strikes the New One World Trade Center as he steps off the plane.
- May 24, 2014 The Pope arrives in Jordan to have a meeting with the Palestinian Authority. At the same moment he arrives, a 4.1 earthquake happens in Israel. An hour later he conducts mass at the Manger Square in Bethlehem and a 6.5 earthquake takes place in Greece at the same moment. At 5:20 PM, Pope Francis is given a throne to sit upon in the historic location of the 'upper room' that is seated over King David's burial tomb. At that moment a rare meteor storm takes place on the east coast of America from a comet called, 'Linear.'
- May 27, 2014, three days after the Pope's message, a fire breaks out in Bethlehem at the Church of the Nativity.

Yes, all these events can be explained away under 'rational thinking.' And yes, lightning often strikes the locations mentioned. But it is also clear that the scriptures make it very clear that we should watch the signs and the times. The repeating instances of lighting, earthquakes, falling statues mixed with locations and demonic blessings can not be ignored.

Biblical standards in the modern 'church.'

Unfortunately there has been a lot of 'cross-pollination' of thought into the Body of Christ from the anti-Christ mindset. And like a ship at sea, it only takes a little mistake early in the voyage to be off a long ways from your destination at the end. Much of the concepts of church structure and dedication to the church system, has forged an extreme loyalty to this lifeless form that so many are dedicated to protect.

Plumb, "Good Behavior"
"Cause perfect only makes you crazy,
there is now way it could save me.
I'm sick of feeling like a traitor,
if this the price for good behavior?"

   The Protestant Church has mirrored many of its practices and policies after Catholic models from the very beginning with Martin Luther's reformation. And today we hold up the ashes of this dead system in every corner and denomination, reinforcing current leadership mindsets of how to 'conduct the ministry.'
   Many within the system protect the 'ministry system' at all costs, even at the expense of the people. How incredibly backwards that is. Once again we have gotten the horse behind the cart and not before it. A true ministry is the by-product of your spiritual life in God, extended to the people as a natural outflow of your life. Not a collection of expendable workers to serve the needs of a leader.
   When the Biblical standards of honor, respect and authority become distorted, soon other issues start to manifest, as the vision of the leadership becomes narrowed and more tunnel-like. Although slowly at first, perhaps even over decades, eventually the church system dances around problems like these.
   Unsafe environments, a heavy-handed performance-driven culture, the over-emphasis on a single leader who becomes the ultimate spokesperson. In so doing the leader's sins become minimized or hidden under the thick cloak of "Speak not against the Lord's anointed!"
   The body in turn starts to feel like it has no place to go. Quiet levels of fear and shame become mixed with manipulation and settle in like silent chains of submission to the church's authority. At this point, people either conform to the "form" they are expected to play. Or they quietly slip out the back door believing themselves to either be on the edge of hell or just a "backslidden sinner" waiting for judgment day.

Unfortunately, and especially in the Charismatic world, a body that has slipped into a performance-based mode now has other problems to deal with. As leadership takes on more and more of the persona of Hollywood, people's desires become twisted and start desiring to become like them.

In order to "conform", people become driven to be like the leaders they see on stage and not pursue a personal relationship with the Lord like they should have been taught. The quest to become a "prophet or apostle" drives them further and further away. They now, unknowingly, open themselves up for anything in the spiritual realm to give them a revelation so that they may 'fit in'. This is where the Kundalini and Jezebel spirits often make their entrance within the body. Within a short amount of time many people are "suddenly" convinced that what they are hearing is the Holy Spirit. Not knowing the Babylonian, anti-Christ system has been re-training them to hear otherwise.

John Mark McMillan, "The Love you Swore."
"Spare my body from the wolves, God.
That crouch down at my door.
Lift me up above the waters.
And the sharks that guard your shore.
'Cause I know that I need you.
But sometimes I know I need you more."

Right now the world is experiencing one continual wave after another of turbulence and destruction fueled by demonic rage. Many pastors of church ministries are adding more and more wood to the fire by declaring that the great tribulation has begun. And yes, this is possible, but I wonder if it's not. It's no great surprise to me and a few others that there are wolves in sheep's clothing running around out there.

There has been in many corners of Christianity over the last few decades, a quiet movement to introduce leaders to various groups of influence. Much of these groups all trace their 'authority' back to the United Nations, the World Council of Churches, or Rome itself. And unfortunately the leadership of many of today's mainline denominations have been absorbed into them.

Even within the Charismatic movement, a 'knighthood' has risen up to absorb many leaders. This knighthood quietly feeds the carnal desires of self-promotion has slowly acquired much of the senior Charismatic leadership of the West. And although this branch of the Knights of Malta claims to be separate from Rome, it fails Jesus' fruit test.

As hard as it may sound to people's ears, the truth is, there is hardly an 'official' place of worship out there that does not have it's spiritual headship compromised. Even some of the most newest faces that have risen in the prophetic world are troubling.

Not long ago, a well-known up-and-coming prophetic pastor in Florida released a prophetic word on the internet that was sent to me. I was part way through the word when I stopped reading it. In the word, he fully admitted that this message came from a demon that entered his room.

Receiving demonic revelation and passing it off as a word from God should be a big red flag to everyone, unfortunately it was not. Not only does this kind of foolish action deceive the young in Christ around them with the image of 'that's ok!' But what also concerned me was the sheer number of Christians around the world who made comments endorsing this behavior on Facebook. Deception is spreading, and our leaders are now blind and following them only leads to a painful end.

So what about all this tribulation stuff? I suspect that what we are seeing is not what we are being told. Events, natural and manmade are being reinterpreted right before our eyes. Mixed with a spirit of fear, they want to make us believe the end times are here.

"He will speak out against the Most High and *wear down the saints* of the Highest One, and he will intend to make alterations in times and in law; and

they will be given into his hand for a time, times, and half a time." (Daniel 7:25 NASB)

Because the devil knows he can not win, one of his tactics is to change the playing field into his favor. By changing the timing of the great tribulation he will increase the body count. Millions if not billions will die and will never have been given a chance to accept Christ's offer. Like the lonely traveler in Pilgrim's progress, the Body of Christ is struggling unknowingly under the burden of the Babylonian system. And, in the eyes of the devil the best time to attack is now by the evidence of what is going on around the world.

Myself, personally I feel that we have some distance yet to cover before the tribulation comes. But as I was told many years ago by the Holy Spirit in the early 1980's, *"that the time before the tribulation will look so much like the tribulation, that people will be deceived into believing that the Great Tribulation has come."*

So get ready. We have a long bumpy road ahead of us, but our King is coming. God wants this on His time table, not the devil's and unfortunately all those who endure these days under the false message will most likely harden their hearts to the real message when it comes.

But it should also be noted the Lord laughs at the devil's plans. **"Why are the nations in an uproar and the peoples devising a vain thing? The kings of the earth take their stand and the rulers take counsel together against the LORD and against His Anointed, saying, "Let us tear their fetters apart and cast away their cords from us!"**

He who sits in the heavens laughs, **The Lord scoffs at them. Then He will**
speak to them in His anger and terrify them in His fury, saying, "But as for me, I have installed My King upon Zion, My holy mountain." (Psalm 2:1-6 NASB)

All these things that have happened both modern and ancient are but the evidence of the small, continual, pernicious shifts that have taken place. Slowly altering the thinking of the Body of Christ with pernicious cultural programming designed to not only disconnect us from the Trinity but each other within the body as well. So let's start moving in the right direction.

A few examples.
Sadly, when leadership starts spiritually slipping off the tracks, arguments are often employed with comments, whispered around the church behind people's backs.

Bitterness.
First of all bitterness is not the same as hardness. And hardness can easily be corrected by God **(Ezekiel 36:26)**
One example often used within church is, "Oh, they're just bitter!" This is often an extremely effective way of quietly discrediting a person who brings up morality issues within a body. But what is true bitterness? Have you ever heard anyone give a sermon on it? Chances are you have not.
First of all, if bitterness was challenging leadership, then the majority of the Old Testament prophets would qualify as bitter who spoke before Kings. And if that were the case, then according to many modern standards implied in Christian circles we should ignore those prophets.
But challenging leadership is not bitterness, nor should we accept some off handed comment from a leader claiming this or that person is. Bitterness is the absence of spiritual sweetness and there are many things that can sour our spirit before God.
"Or do you not know that unrighteous individuals will not inherit God's kingdom? Stop being deceived; neither fornicators nor idolaters nor adulterers nor those who are of a voluptuous nature, given to the gratification of sensual, immoral appetites, neither men who are guilty of sexual intercourse with members of their own sex, nor thieves, nor those who are always greedy to have more than they possess, nor drunkards, nor revivers, nor extortioners, shall inherit God's kingdom." (1 Corinthians 6:9-10 WET.)

The fact is, if we are living a life pleasing to God, then we are a sweet aroma before him. And is that not what really counts?

But let's take a closer look at the subject itself. Many subjects within scripture can be examined closer by looking at its equivalent within Biblical symbolism. One of the strongest symbols for sweetness is honey. This is a complex and wonderful symbol that has two sides to it.

Honey often is a sign of delight because of its sweetness, and everything sweet in the natural world often corresponds to what is delightful and pleasant in the spiritual world. This is because Honey is seen as a blessing, scripture, wisdom and anointing. **"How sweet are Your words to my taste! Yes, sweeter than honey to my mouth!" (Psalm 119:103 NASB).**

But it is also connected to Judgement and Repentance. **Matthew 3:4, Mark1:6, Rev10:9-10, Ezekiel 3:3**

Because of sweetness's connection with wisdom and the word in general, sweetness in my opinion is therefore connected with Truth, and truth has two sides to it **(Hebrews 4:12)** It cuts, divides and separates. To the righteous it brings delight but to others it is harsh and judgmental because truth exposes all things to the light.

That is why so many people with a correctional word can be perceived as harsh and bitter. Because it exposes the dark, and so is painful to them. This is one of the many reasons to make sure you are right before God when you deliver the message.

The Lord's Anointed.

The few that decide to stand up and call leadership to account are minimized under a series of cultural verbiage designed to discredit them into silence. Forgetting the understanding that anyone who has been redeemed under Christ's blood is now anointed.

A division is created when we accept the argument of "speak not against the Lord's anointed". The reality is that we are all on the same playing field, and you and I have the same right and anointing to bring up morality issues to a leader as any leader does of you.

For if both of you are anointed, then you are not 'less' or 'higher' than the leader. And you have just as much right under Heaven to bring up issues of morality within a Biblical context.

It was in the early days of the Vineyard, at one of John Wimber's Canadian meetings, that I heard him say something I have never forgotten. *"If you are unwilling to accept correction from even the newest child in Christ, then you've got a problem."* This is very true because we all have been given the same measure of the Holy Spirit, and now that the Trinity lives within us, God can speak through anyone, just ask Balaam.

The Son of God was so approachable and welcoming to sinners and children. I would like to suggest that if people are intimidated by a leader's presence, then the presence you're feeling is not the Holy Spirit, and it should be a red flag to you.

Religious Spirit.

One other thing that is often tossed out to discredit the message is the comment that, "they have a religious spirit!" The ambiguity of this statement is often hard to define, this is mainly because scripture talks far more about lawlessness than legalism. With very little clearly defined Biblical attributes to identify legalism, a clear definition of what could be legalism (Religious Spirit) is now totally subject to a person's perspective of who said it.

True freedom in Christ to do or not to do, is all under the direction of the Holy Spirit. And I have personally found that some people use the accusation of, "they have a religious spirit", as a way of deflecting people's attention from their personal lawlessness.

Yes, true legalism does exist. But like the biblical examples found in scripture, talking more about lawlessness than legalism. It seems to me there are far more examples of lawless Christians running around than legalistic ones. True legalism is about control, domination, and power. And in its ultimate form tolerates no one.

If we were to be totally honest with ourselves then we would need to admit we have all dipped our toes in that pool at one point or another. The problem only intensifies as demonic spirits start influencing and pushing our desires for 'correctness' to satisfy our perceived and twisted understanding of personal holiness. Great examples of this exist in scripture when the Pharisees became offended with Jesus' answers, claiming he was the Son of Man. Their inflexible tapestries of stone had blinded them from the Holy of Holies who stood before them.

Often the immature cannot tell the difference and misunderstand the

distinction between people's personal convictions and religious inflexibility. As a result, these things often get lumped into the same mix. In Romans 14, Paul uses the example of food to highlight an important point concerning our freedom in Christ. All of this is totally built on the foundational understanding of our personal relationship with the Trinity.

This same argument Paul delivers can be completely adapted to many other situations, like having a television or not. Or even if a person celebrates a certain holiday or not. We all walk with God at the best speed our feeble legs can travel. Don't judge someone if they hobble or skip a beat. This is because we all have 'issues'. And whether or not you're ignorant of yours, everyone one else can often see them.

"But as for you, why are you judging your brother? Or, as for you also, why are you treating your brother with contempt?" (Romans 14:10 WET). Because Lawlessness is the opposite side of the road of Legalism, both should be examined with each other. Each side seems to have its protected absolutes that the mind builds trenches and fortifications around. Legalism must have its 'perfect correctness' while lawlessness seems to build a protective quagmire around it with the motto, 'because all things are permissible in Christ'.

Legalism strips away a lot of the mysteries and joy-filled wonder of God (not to mention friendships) to be replaced with a vending machine thinking of cause and effect. What you put in is what you get out, as you tremble before the angry god.

Lawlessness feeds your old nature and eventually justifies all your sinful actions under a watered down understanding of grace, that has neutered the holiness of God living in you.

As such things are embraced, the next up and coming generation is rendered ineffective as they model the actions of their teachers. Each new generation stands up, or learns to walk away from what they are seeing. In this tug-of-war, the spiritual salt of people's lives either becomes calcified into stone or so contaminated with spiritual pollutants that it is thrown out. **"As for you, you are the salt of the earth. But if the salt loses its pungency, by what means can it's saltiness be restored? For not even one thing is it of use any longer, except, having been thrown out, to be trampled underfoot by men." Matthew 5:13 WET.**

Such a lack of Spiritual salt causes a weakness to the heart, a kind of Dilated Cardiomyopathy *(your heart muscle is too weak to pump blood efficiently. The muscles stretch and become thinner. This allows the chambers of your heart to expand)*. As a result, the spring of Living Water is no longer pumped through you to keep you fresh and living. This is the after-effects of mushy grace lawlessness that has no boundaries. Eventually without borders to protect your spiritual heart, it expands until it can no longer be of use.

Either of these choices is not really an option. Unfortunately we have all most likely walked in one or even both of these two areas at some point in our history. I've done it and, if you're honest with yourself, you have done it as well. And I am willing to bet that at some point in the future you and I will do it again. Stone hearts can be made soft again, **(Ezekiel 36:26)** and old worn-out hearts can be made strong once more as the Lord calls us to remember His acts of the past.

There are, unfortunately, many levels of problems within the Lord's body. Over time, even the smallest of them can cause problems as they add layers for us to work through. Some are just simply a simplistic understanding of issues that the devil can exploit. Let's explore one issue that truly needs to be explored far deeper that most of us have heard.

The Power of Headship.

Many years ago, in the 1980s, my wife had become the director of the missions program for a small Baptist church. At one point she found herself more and more uncomfortable with giving money to certain groups, even though she did not know why.

At her request I started looking into these groups and how they tied to the denomination that church was connected to, American Baptist. Searching primarily the main website of that denomination I soon found its connection to larger groups, The World Council of Churches and the National Council of Churches. The more I dug, the more I did not like, so we compiled the given information and called a meeting with all the people connected with the missions program to discuss the information.

An odd sequence of events quickly took place in that meeting. Very quickly it was like we were watching unfold a living example of the cartoon of the three monkeys. "Hear no evil, see no evil, speak no evil."

Just starting the meeting you could almost see people's minds close off as they quickly decided that they did not want to hear the information being presented. To them it was enough that something was found and they were willing to stop all funds to these organizations without any evidence.

Then, almost as if some spirit within the church was hitting the panic button, the church janitor stepped around the corner with his face as white as a sheet. He vanished as quickly as he came in and less than ten seconds later the pastor quickly entered the room. He asked what was going on, we explained and he admitted that he already knew all the stuff we were trying to present.

At that moment it was all about damage control by the pastor, with a bit of back-peddling before the group we had assembled. In the end he agreed that funds would no longer be sent to these groups.

Over the next few months, many older people were glad of what we had done. However they all quickly shut down the conversation if we attempted to explain any details. That seemed extremely odd to us, for how can you avoid repeating the same problem like this if you don't know what to look for?

That, however, was only the start of the tapestry coming apart as other facts wandered in, painting a new picture in my mind of what had happened years ago with the former pastor. A suspicion that was later confirmed by a meeting with some of the former elders of the church. The former pastor had been trying to get the church out of the denomination for some of the very same reasons we had discovered. **"Evil companionships corrupt good morals." 1 Corinthians 15:33 WET**

So how is all this connected? The World Council of Churches creation seems to have a lot of vague connections in the beginning. The modern retelling of the story now seems to be highly "cleaned up" compared to what I remember reading in the 80's.

However it is believed and reported by many, that the KGB in the 60s and the 80s influenced many of its elections. This would probably help explain why former WCC leader, Emilio Castro, who had an apparently pro-Communist attitude gave some odd remarks in 1971 concerning the African National Congress (ANC) and the Southwest African People's Organization (SWAPO). These Communist groups were practicing a horrific form of killing called "necklacing." Butchering around 600 of their own people, they cut off the hands and then lit a rubber tire on fire that was fixed around the neck. Emilio's comment on it was, *"a painful but minor expression of their resistance, it is an injustice to label this as violence!"*

But let's look at some other points of interest.
 1. February 1991, Canberra Australia. 4000 people gather at the 7th World Assembly with Dr. Chung Hyun-Kyung. Ms. Chung, a Presbyterian minister in Korea and a professor at Ewha Woman's University in Seoul. Dr. Hyun-Kyung invited the audience to participate in a ritual dance. This sensual dance was a part of the preparation ritual intended to *"prepare the way for the spirits. To invoke the spirits of the dead"*
 2. During this meeting they produced a guideline publication for worship, in it the following names were suggested for worship. The Source, Lady of peace, Lady of wisdom, Lady of love, Lady of birth, Lord of stars, Lord of planets, Mother, Home, Baker woman, Presence, Power, Essence, Simplicity.
 3. November 1993, Minneapolis Minnesota. 2000 women gathered for the "Re Imaging Conference" with the following speakers, Chung Hyun-Kyung, Virginia Mollenkott, Elizabeth Bettenhausen, Lois Wilson and Jose Hobday. Here is a few quotes from the conference.
 ~"I don't' think we need a theory of atonement at all. I think Jesus came for life and to show us something about life. I don't think we need folks hanging on crosses and blood dripping and weird stuff ... we just need to listen to the God within."~ *Delores Williams of Union Theological Seminary*
 ~"My bowel is Buddhist bowel, my heart is Buddhist heart, my right brain is Confucian brain, and my left brain is Christian brain."~*Virginia Mollenkott*
 ~"When we do trance healing, we believe that this life-giving energy came from god and it is everywhere, it is in the sun, in the ocean, from the ground and it is from the trees ... We ask god's permission to use this life-giving energy for our sisters and brothers in need. If you feel very tired and you don't have any energy to

give, what you do is ... go to a big tree and ask it to `give me some of your life energy" ~ *Dr. Chung Hyun-Kyung*

4. The Minneapolis Star Tribune also reported the following, "throughout the conference worship experiences will celebrate Sophia, the biblical goddess of creation."

So how does this affect headship?

Unfortunately if you do a quick search on the subject of headship for your own personal study you will find most of it centered under the "umbrella" concept of a wife's submission to her husband. This is only one aspect and, in my opinion, represents a very narrow view.

The reality is **"And *all things* He put in subjection under His feet, and Him He gave as Head over all things to the Assembly, which is of such a nature as to be His body, the fulness of the One who constantly is filling all things with all things." (Ephesians 1:22-23 WET).**

All things really means *all things*. And the things and people that you and I sit under can have a powerful effect on your life for either good or bad. It is well known that through the sin of Adam, all creation groans under the weight or effect of sin. Why?

The reason for this is very simple, after God created Man he put all of creation under him. That is what we call today, headship. That is, the head authority guiding the ship, head-ship. That is also why the devil wanted Jesus to submit under him. Jesus refused and as a result a new order of things is being established.

All things that are truly under Jesus will in time reflect His character just as all things under the devil reflect his. This is the true value of understanding the parable of the fruit tree. By testing the fruit, we know the headship of what we are looking at. Now just as children are a reflection of their parents, which is one of the reasons behind **Titus 1:6** as a qualification of an Elder, a congregation is a reflection of the leader.

This is because whatever the leader carries spiritually

good or bad is the path the people follow. Now I know I just put a serious amount of pressure on the leaders, and this is partly true. But the other half of this falls in the laps of the congregation. This is because in a community, spiritual things are shared by all.

Let me give an example or two from things I have seen. In many places I have traveled, if the pastor walks in the prophetic it will not be long until many others start doing the same. Now this is not isolated to just this gift. My writing exploded after becoming a member of an organization where the head leader is known for writing a lot of books.

On the other hand it's not uncommon in churches to find certain widespread chronic problems like alcoholism, anger, drug abuse and things like this around them. Believe it or not, this is often an issue within headship. What this means for the congregation is the elders need to carry the senior leadership in prayer when they see this. Just as the congregation needs to carry the elders above them in prayer. Remember, 'blessings come down as prayers go up'. It's a cycle.

Learn the cycle and if the Body of Christ learns to peddle this bicycle well, we will all move forward. Why elders? Because elders biblically are the spiritual and physical gatekeepers of the congregation and they should have the maturity of years to carry this with grace. These things do not always require confrontation, especially if there is no obvious evidence.

"One another's burdens be constantly bearing, and thus you will fully satisfy the requirements of the law of the Christ." (Galatians 6:2 WET). Like a runaway beast, sin will run over the top of your brother leaving him "overtaken in sin." These trampled leaders are often wounded, possibly embarrassed. So the elders of the congregation have a duty to carry the leader in prayer until such time they can be restored without manipulative pressure. This is why headship is so important and this is also why the Body needs to divorce themselves from the Babylonian system. How can you help someone when its headship is of the devil? With a lot of care, I think.

Now as I have hinted at earlier in the book, and started to explore now, most denominations and groups are now highly intertwined in larger groups above them. And those groups have a connection that keeps funneling upward. It is assumed that such connections are for Kingdom building, cooperation, and 'ecumenical reasons,' so the average believer does not look any deeper. The fact is, these connections in one way or another all find their way to Rome. Fulfilling the truth in the old saying, "all roads lead to Rome."

Doing a bit of research, a person will quickly find that nearly every denomination in the world today has a strong connection to the World Council of Churches. But since the chances are most of the readers of this book will be from America I will focus on just that list.

Evangelical Alliance
African Methodist Episcopal Zion Church [USA]
American Baptist Churches in the USA
Anglican Church of Canada
Apostolic Catholic Assyrian Church of the East, N.A. Diocese Canadian Council of Churches
Canadian Yearly Meeting of the Religious Society of Friends Christian Church (Disciples of Christ) in Canada
Christian Church (Disciples of Christ)
Christian Methodist Episcopal Church [USA]
Church of the Brethren [USA]
Episcopal Church
Estonian Evangelical Lutheran Church Abroad [Canada] Evangelical Lutheran Church in America
Evangelical Lutheran Church in Canada
Hungarian Reformed Church in America
International Council of Community Churches [USA]
International Evangelical Church [USA]
Moravian Church in America
National Baptist Convention of America

National Baptist Convention, USA, Inc.
National Council of the Churches of Christ in the USA
Orthodox Church in America
Polish National Catholic Church
Presbyterian Church in Canada
Presbyterian Church (USA)
Progressive National Baptist Convention, Inc. [USA]
Reformed Church in America [USA]
Religious Society of Friends [USA] United Church of Canada
United Church of Christ [USA] United Methodist Church [USA]

   Focusing on just one group in the list, the Evangelical Alliance website shows an impressive list of 128 evangelical groups that are well known in the Body of Christ. Now, I would assume most of these groups built these connections out of the desire to build the Kingdom and expand the Gospel. Not realizing what they had connected themselves to. But as I related in our own experience from the 80s, I am also sure that there are a few out there who know the *real truth* as well.

   Coming under the headship, knowingly or unknowingly, of evil creates a spiritual problem. **"I will not give My glory to another, Nor My praise to idols." (Isaiah 42:8 NASB).** This is because God not only does not share well, and to do so is an offense to Him. These things are highlighted in the story of Nadab and Abihu **(Leviticus 10)** as well as the story of Ananias and Sapphira **(Acts 5)**

   I cannot understate the value of quality headship. Just as you cannot learn a skill like carpentry while working for an electrician. Your revelatory gifting will crawl and not excel if the local headship is not operating in that. You will however expand in other areas that the local leadership carries, either good or bad. The truth is, if you want to experience the light, you need to go where it is shining, because a garden does not grow well in darkness.

I can easily attribute many of the spiritual tools in my tool belt to some of the ministries I have been connected with. I can also attribute many of the negative things around me to some of the same ministries.

Consider the original twelve apostles. Rough men, some of questionable character, sat for three years under the King of Eternity, building relationships in a community of friendship that defined their very foundation, and was continually being shaped and softened by the Holy Spirit until their death.

Like a burr under the saddle of a horse, what filters down in headship from Rome to our local congregations is the hidden background noise that keeps the well of our souls in perpetual irritation.

The larger picture.

As previously mentioned when I quoted **2 Corinthians 2:11**, God does not want us to be unaware of the devil's plans. Since the days of Nimrod, the Anti-Christ spirit has used assimilation of local religions as a battle tactic. This worked well for the most part until the coming of Christ's assemblies.

Just as Christ crucified was a stumbling block to the religious order of his day **(1 Corinthians 1:23)**, the Father's household became a stumbling block and foolishness to the Roman Empire.

And in my opinion assimilation was used once more as a tactic for the survival of the priesthood. Rome worked hard to enforce this concept as the Christians for the next few hundred years did not give in, forcing the new Babylon to change tactics once again. With demonic orders disguised as coming from heaven they released the armies and started butchering on a large scale.

In some ways this worked, but ultimately it backfired as Christians started "feeling" a strong need to rebel and secure a home for themselves. Christian armies rose up to challenge the power of Rome as early Protestantism struggled against Rome and, unfortunately, in time each other, to define what true freedom in Christ was.

With the opening of the "New World" the tactics of

Rome flipped once again. With no real power in these new nations they came in with a helping hand to help with the widows, orphans, and the "lost" tribal people of the new world. Harvesting, killing, and subduing in silence they took away much of the spiritual harvest under the concept of "fair play."

Eventually, in a quiet, pernicious way they reenacted the old policy of assimilation silently at the end of the 1940's with the creation of the World Council of Churches. Working in silence seems to be the new tactic used as this ancient demonic order slowly wrapping the vines of the world around our feet. Compartmentalizing our world into increasingly smaller networks so that we see no other possibilities.

"I Go to prepare a place for you".

"In My Father's House are many mansions; if it were not so, I would have told you. I go to prepare a place for you, I will come again and receive you unto myself, that where I am, there you may be also."

"So then faith comes by hearing and hearing by the word of God."

My Father's House
Chapter Four
Whispers of the Promised Land

"I will bring you to the land which I swore to give to Abraham, Isaac, and Jacob, and I will give it to you for a possession; I am the Lord."

"You will seek Me and find Me when you search for Me with all your heart."

"Ask, and it will be given to you; seek, and you will find; knock, and it will be opened to you. For everyone who asks receives, and he who seeks finds, and to him who knocks it will be opened."

"THE SPIRIT OF MAN IS THE LAMP OF THE LORD, SEARCHING ALL THE INNERMOST PARTS OF HIS BEING."

"HIS DISCIPLES REMEMBERED THAT IT WAS WRITTEN, "ZEAL FOR YOUR HOUSE WILL CONSUME ME."

Elissa Yoder, "Misfit."
"So I rise from the dust of yesterday.
Dead man stays in his grave.
I am striking the match, and walking away.
This house was made to be burned.
Erased from the skyline, rewrite my time line.
No shadow will darken me now,
No shadow will darken me now."

As I stated in Chapter Two, *"To begin to fully understand the mess of this present age, we need to become aware of a few spiritual realities that few teach on these days."* Let me condense some of this down with some information that we all need that other people have noted.

When Christianity started in the Middle East, it started as a Fellowship.
-Then it moved to Greece and it became a Philosophy.
-Moving to Italy it became an Institution.
-In Europe it transitioned into a Culture,
-But in America, it became an Enterprise.

An *Enterprise* is another word for a for-profit making *business* or company. In other words, its purpose is to make money. So think about this, Christ's bride is being used to make money. Yes, that's **prostitution.**
It's no wonder so many of us in "church" feel disconnected or used spiritually, a relationship with a prostitute is artificial and only exists as long as we continue putting dollar bills in her hand.
Thereby creating a mindset within the body that relationship is based on what we give the church/god. And not based on the reality of adoption into a family. Spiritual prostitution is always based on performance and turns you and your relationship with God and the church into a commodity. And as a commodity all your outward stuff like dress, speech and actions are measured closely to see if your outward "appeal" is pleasing to the system

that demands a performance.

Adoption is a family, lover, friend mindset that can grow in natural ways and will always focus our thoughts towards the inward issues. Things like character, integrity and honesty become less of a "badge of honor" and more of a personal foundation as the Holy Spirit builds the tapestry of your life with Faith, Hope and Love.

Unfortunately much of our modeling of how the Body of Christ is to be run has been distorted by the yeast of the Babylonian church systems that has filtered in during the early centuries. The precious few Apostolic communities of the Celtic and Waldensian have long faded in their effectiveness, leaving us with only shadows of a life that once existed.

Some things, of course, can be gleaned for inspiration from the pages and notes of their history, keeping in mind that even this history has been distorted by later catholic writers. To fill in the void of understanding will require the Holy Spirit to fill in our absence of understanding in order to restore some measure of true life. Therefore I will include some breadcrumbs I have found along the way for us all to ponder and reflect on.

> *"Christianity is not a commodity, you can't sell Christ,"*
> *~ Rich Mullins.*

Breadcrumbs

"The thief does not come except to steal and to kill and destroy. I alone came in order that they might be possessing life, and that they might be possessing it in superabundance." (John 10:10 WET).

Super-abundance is a promise, and the pernicious plan of the enemy has slowly displaced the Body of Christ away from the feast of the promise set before us. We can see the promise ahead and a few of us dare to hope in the aroma of the food at the end of the tunnel. But unfortunately we have waited so long, that the moss and grass have grown around our feet like chains, making us believe that we just need to settle where we are and consider ourselves blessed for what little we have.

Few break away and stop listening to the words of centuries of social conditioning that have filled us with fears of the unknown. But, as a well known Christian speaker in Texas by the name of Curry Blake once said, "Your happiness should not live in someone else's head!"

The reality is, so very much of our understanding is upside down. Many corners of modern Christianity have so cannibalized and twisted the basic spiritual concepts that when we hear them, we unknowingly take them out of context to make them mean what we think we have been taught. Like Pavlov's dog, we drool out preconditioned teaching like a vending machine as soon as certain words or ideas are brought to us.

All the while in secret we slowly become more and more discontent with the status quo as our hunger for more slowly eats at our soul.

Margaret Becker, "The Hunger Stays."
"...I've been thinking about what I've been through,
All the good times, all the bad,
And anywhere in between the two
there runs a common thread.
Some call it a condition,
A hidden chasm that will never fill up.
A constant thirst for Your presence, A longing for Your love.

The hunger stays, I keep on reaching.
The hunger stays, I keep on seeking.
The hunger stays through the blessing,

through the bleeding, the hunger stays.
I've seen Your rivers in my desert,
Seen Your miracles time after time.
And when I think I can't take anymore,
I see there's so much more to find."

In my personal quest to hit the reset button, the hunger has driven me to look at many different things. At one point I re-examined the idea of re-joining the Vineyard only to realize the Lord was not pointing that way. Local churches held nothing for us as I would sit in the back, arms crossed, realizing that not only had I seen this show before, but I could also predict, without any special spiritual gift, the entire service.

I had enough of preaching and worship shows. People smiled, said nice things and then next week they gave you the same look of "oh a new person" all over again.

I, in some ways, had become 'spoiled' by the Christian friends I left behind in the South. In that environment, the friendship and community seemed to always be growing no matter what craziness the third floor had thrown down at us. FYI: the third floor was senior management who often made our efforts and life more difficult.

One of the ways the Lord has often driven me in certain directions is by the environment He builds around me. For some time, many different things would "pop up" concerning Ireland. Then eventually friends of ours moved to Ireland as missionaries. During this time I ran into a song from a band called, "Iona." Listening to many songs, some I liked, others did not, I heard the song, "Encircling."

Amazed I thought, "wow, those are powerful Apostolic declarations!" Not realizing until after I investigated further that they were actually the words of Patrick, over a thousand years before.

Iona, "Encircling"
LORICA
"I bind unto myself today, The power of God to hold and lead. His eye to watch, His might to stay, His ear to hearken to my need. The wisdom of my God to teach, His hand to guide His shield to ward. The word of God to give me speech, His heavenly host to be my guard.
TARA
The wisdom of my God to teach, His hand to guide His shield to ward. The word of God to give me speech, His heavenly host to be my guard.
CAIM
The Mighty Three, My protection Be. Encircling me."

Knowing what little I did from a historical point of view, I dug a little deeper. Only to discover that these apostolic training centers of the early Celtic church had a very deep, rich life. The majority of these students lived around eighteen years at these places before becoming "commissioned" and sent out. When the community of Iona was created in 563 AD, two hundred people left with Colum Cille 'Columba' to build that community.

When Aidan left Iona to build Lindisfarne, he did not do it alone, but with twelve other missionaries. These thoughts kept wandering around my mind as other things entered, like the phrase out of the song, *"The Mighty Three, My protection be."*

Researching Celtic Christianity, I ran across this little gem of information from Trevor Miller of the Northumbria Community.

"The emphasis on the Trinity cannot be overstated. It's always good to remind ourselves as Christians, that Community began in the heart of God. That the self sufficient God who is love, is Community within Himself. And that all Community flows from this."

Also from Trevor Miller.

"The early Celtic Northumbrian spirituality had a profound understanding of this. One of their prayers stated, 'God is Father, Son and Spirit. Therefore God is Three in One. Therefore God is Community. If we are made in the image of God, Then we will find our fulfillment in Community (in relationships of love)."

When I ran across this it was one of those 'light bulb moments' as other things I had read all started flowing together as one stream of thought.

"And as for myself, the glory which you have given me, I have given them, in order that they might be one even as we are one, I in them and you in me, in order that they, having been brought to a state of completeness with respect to oneness, may persist in that state of completeness, to the end of the world might be understanding that you sent me on a mission and

that you loved them even as you loved me." (John 17:19-21 WET).

Consider this, in the lingering traces of this ancient Apostolic community, the teaching of the Trinity was central to all things. We encircled the Trinity and the Trinity encircled us. Because, in the community we were meant to be so intermixed with the fellowship of the Trinity that the concept of separation was inconceivable. All things in community life grew out of that understanding. It was far, far more than the watered down teaching of today that imparts the idea that we are the representatives of Christ to the earth.

Simply put, this modern teaching is incomplete and gives a perception of being 'alone.' Rather we walk forward with many unseen around us. For a true representation of the Holy to a fallen world to take place, an experiential knowledge that only comes from living in the presence of God is required. Otherwise, how can we be representatives of something we have no experience of?

Consider this short excerpt from *Foxe's Book of Martyrs* during the reign of Emperor Gallus (251-253) who was later killed by his own soldiers. *"Most of the errors which crept into the Church at this time arose from placing human reason in competition with revelation."* True revelation not only comes from God, but is also carried in the common union of the experience of fellowship.

Because errors crept in, it is also recorded during this time the following, *"it was unfortunate for the Gospel, that many errors had, about that time crept into the Church: the Christians were at variance with each other; self-interest divided those whom social love ought to have united; and the virulence of pride occasioned a variety of factions."*

At this point the outside world saw the Christian community splitting apart. They seized the opportunity and drastically increased its persecution of Christians. The experiential relationship we had with the Trinity and each other was replaced with human reasoning and we lost.

The reality is that, according to John 17, the world will

understand once they see the love of God resting on the community. The community was designed to be a testimony to the world. That's what it means when it says' **"...the world might be understanding..."**

The Father, the Son and the Holy Spirit exist in constant community and through the blood sacrifice of the Son. We, the household of God, are invited into a very large community. We are invited into The Father's House, a house not made by hands. But held together by the common bonds of blood, fellowship, love and joy. That is why the dream I had, strongly emphasized to me three times that the LORD will build My Father's House.

No human hands can do it, we can speak it, we can pray it, we can live and exist in it, but He must build it. The corporation of the church offers service to the system in the name of Jesus. Jesus, the living Hope, offers life abundant in the garden of your soul with the Trinity.

The gospel of the church is to come, participate, serve the system so that we may all enter heaven together.

The Gospel of the Kingdom offers, **"I alone came in order that they might be possessing life, and that they might be possessing it in superabundance. I alone am the good shepherd, the good one." (John 10:10-11 WET)**. That means that the Kingdom starts here, now, in the center of our soul, not at some future point. For all of God's promises are "Yes," towards us **1 Corinthians 1:20.**

Some may call this splitting hairs, but in reality it is one of the small shifts of thinking that has so easily pointed the people of God away from our journey to a system.

So let's start the process of stripping away the 'old things' that so easily entangle us from moving forward. And as we do, I would like to say that what is written within this book is not meant to be a step by step plan or guide of rules for a person to follow. For as we take the journey to step away from the mindset of the institutions and corporations of the church. We should seek the wild waters of this frontier to embrace a spiritual life that we have only dreamed about. It should be noted that you will find it very hard to get more than one person to agree on what Christian Spirituality is. So I encourage you to turn your face into the wind, and not be burdened with 'getting it right'.

The Power of True Worship.
There is a reality that we all know about worship that is in conflict with the implied conditioning that the system whispers in our ear. We all know, or at least I should hope we all know, that worship can happen anywhere and does not require a location. The system however implies a subtle message, that to have true worship it must be in an official building at the leading of the anointed person on the stage.

So here is a question for pondering: John the Baptist spent years in the desert alone. Was he wrong to be isolated? After all he was the fore-runner of Christ to make the way. Was his worship in the desert invalid or somehow weak because he was alone? Was Paul out of line for spending fourteen years in the desert receiving revelation with no one to test it on?

Consider Jesus' words to the woman at the well. **"Be believing me, woman, there comes an hour when neither in this mountain nor in Jerusalem will you worship the Father." (John 4:21 WET).** In other words it is not about a physical location, it is about higher things.

Because, in the end the only thing that really matters will be; **"But there comes an hour and is now, when the *genuine worshippers* shall worship the Father in a spiritual sphere, and in the sphere of truth. For indeed, the Father is seeking such as these who worship Him. God as to His nature is spirit..." (John 4:23 WET).**

That means the guilt of social conditioning so many feel about not gathering in an official location is just a pointless trick on our minds. Your bathroom is just as valid as your car or beside the crib as you rock your child.

Special Standing.
The Babylonian system that has permeated the Body of Christ over the centuries has been in place so long that even the desire to get away and find the real truth is challenged by our own flawed understanding. As a result, it will take many hours of group pondering over things "we think we know" to find the real bedrock of understanding.

In doing this we will face many pitfalls along the way. One temptation is to try and turn our new findings into a new system of rules to follow. We simply cannot replace one system of rules and laws for another. This is because the true fruit of the Spirit in our lives is meant to be self-governing. The first century church fought over this and it was most likely at the heart of the disagreement between Paul and Peter.

It appears to me as if Peter was slipping into old patterns of thinking, resulting in Paul challenging Peter concerning his hypocrisy of not associating with Gentile believers. There is no longer any Jew or Gentile in Christ, all special standings have been eliminated and any preconceived class system is gone.

The Anti-Christ, Babylonian system creates subtle divisions in our minds. And once that is in place, it continues to find other ways of dividing even those groups more. The Kingdom creates a family, a community and says "Hey, join me at the table." It does this by flipping the religious system on its head. The first becomes last and last becomes first. You may have thought this or that person will have some special standing because of anointing or current earthly position.

But what man holds in high honor, the Lord often ignores and as a result the lowest person in human eyes will get to be close to the Lord. Take a close look at the attributes of those Jesus called 'blessed' in his Sermon on the Mount. This is an attitude of the heart, not a system of laws.

Relics.

One of the incredible twisted divisions in the last two thousand years has been the idea of 'Relics'. Relics are often body parts of people who either walked in some spiritual power or were of a special class. The basic idea is everybody gets a body part to put on display in their church, thereby making their church special. As twisted and morbid this may sound to modern ears, we have our own collection of relics, although not as morbid.

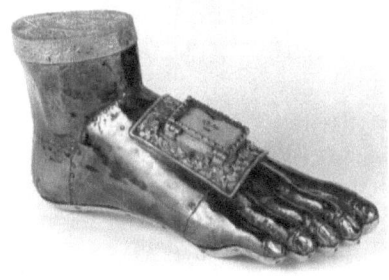

It is clear in **Leviticus 2:11**, that even priests would have been considered "unclean" if they dealt with body parts. So why should body parts (Relics) be brought into the center of our meetings?

Ever heard the old saying, "only he could mess up a free lunch!" God has given us everything we need, yet we still try to find ways to elevate things to a special status and eventually worship it in the place of God himself.

This is probably one of the main reasons the Israelites were told not to make any graven images. As silly as this may sound to our modern ears, consider this scenario. Jesus was a carpenter before he started preaching. What do you think people would do, how would they react if someone dug up some of his woodwork? Let alone his tax records that every Jew had to pay to the Roman government with his signature on it? It would be treated as the 'most holy' artifact in existence.

The reality is it was just a bit of woodworking, nothing more, nothing less. And if it supplanted people's worship of him, then I would hope Jesus would destroy it like he ordered in the Old Testament when people went nuts with the snake that was lifted up on the pole.

Today, we have done the same in many ways with our buildings, wooden crosses and bibles. Some group claiming to work in exorcism will grab a bible for each hand and shake it at the demon like a talisman or magical charm to ward off the demon. Really?

Demons don't leave because you shake a Bible in your hand. Demons leave because of the authority Christ has given you throughout the blood. And that authority is the only thing respected. Today we treat many of the "things of the church" like talisman or charms hoping for a spiritual outcome. We have ignored the greater and celebrated the lesser.

Symbols

Our world is full of them. Bibles are information meant for the transformation into Christlikeness just as holiness is the evidence of fruit from a changed life. Each in its own way is a symbol of something greater. A collection of alphabetic symbols assembled correctly form a word, and that word often represents more than one symbol in your mind. This is why a picture is worth a thousand words.

Cross of Lorraine

The collection of Christian symbols is vast, some are good, some unfortunately have gotten mixed with occult symbols. An example would be the double cross of Lorraine. Used by the Templars and found on Oreo cookies, it was also seen in Sumeria. It was a symbol of Heraldry for Rene D'Anjou and Charles Peguy to represent the blood of both Christ and Satan mixed together.

As a result many occult groups embrace it as one of their own symbols.

Plain wooden crosses are a symbol, like a sign post along the road. When our brothers and sisters in the past used wooden crosses, it was a declaration to the spiritual realm that the Kingdom had arrived and all demonic forces would now be subject to the new orders of the Father's children. Laying a cross on a person and seeing them get healed was like planting a flag on a foreign soil, declaring, "we have come!"

When older believers hundreds of years ago walked into a town with the cross. It told every demon that the Army of the Lord had arrived, and that is the true reality of such powerful symbols. But even the greatest of these symbols are pointless and powerless if the temple of the Lord (that's you!) are not at least trying to live the life Jesus has for you. As a result of such weakness the temptation to use them like a talisman becomes very strong.

But nowadays many have defaulted to the mental concept that there is power in the symbols themselves, turning them into idols. And in their ignorance, they've forgotten that the power does not reside in things made by human hands, but in the life Christ has redeemed by His blood. You can not turn symbols into idols. This, unfortunately, is just another division the Anti-Christ system has created to divorce the Children of God from their rightful bread.

Who are we?

In this book I have, seemingly inconsistently, used the word 'church' at times and at other times I used terms like, 'The Body of Christ, Fellowship, Congregation or Assembly.' This was not an accident, but planned as the 'church' is not the same as the rest.

In 1597 AD, a pagan king compiled together a series of teachings on the demonic world calling the book, "Daemonologie." It covered many dark subjects including the classification of demons, witches, sorcery, werewolves, necromancy (the use of human body parts like brains and eyes) and much, much more. **"for it is disgraceful even to speak of the things which are done by them in secret." (Ephesians 5:12 NASB).**

The fruit of this book, although written under the idea of exposing darkness, actually has helped to encourage the growth and spread of darkness over the centuries.

Shakespeare apparently used it in the creation of his play, 'Macbeth'. In more recent times many claim it inspired the creation of the board game *Dungeons and Dragons* as well.

Then in 1611 AD, this same pagan king, King James ordered the assembly of the Bible. When he did, he ordered the scholars to substitute the word 'church' in the place of 'assembly.' The very nature of the word, 'church' automatically draws the reader's attention to the building. Whereas the term 'assembly' draws the reader's thinking to the people. This simple change helped to mentally and quietly draw the peoples' thinking away from each other to a closer connection to the institution. Nearly every translation since that time has included the word 'church.'

This problem only served as a foundation for future errors in other translations, extremely watering down the effectiveness of the words of God. Today the Holy respect of His words are often shuffled aside if a person does not like what they are reading. That is until they find another version of the Bible that pacifies the tension the Holy Spirit was using to bring correction to their lives.

This is because we, the Body of Christ are ALWAYS in the process of transition from what we are, to who we are to become. Conviction is one of the God-given processes for this. Do not abort this new life. **"For who has shown contempt for the day of small things?..." (Zechariah 4:10 NASB).** All these things are the new seeds that are to grow in the new garden He is building within you.

But that is a subject for the next book. Let's get back to the main subject. Fortunately in the mid nineteenth and twentieth centuries a few scholars started the process of reclaiming the lost ground. Kenneth Wuest created the Wuest Expanded Translation New Testament, (WET), James Darby assembled the Darby translation, (DBY). All of these corrected *most* of the errors of the original King James Version.

The word 'church' pre-existed long before Christ's

sacrifice on the cross. The word, 'church' is an offshoot of the word "Circe or circle" and is a direct connection to the name of a Greek goddess by the name of "Circe." Circe was the daughter of Hecate, the goddess of sorcery. And by extension Circe was known for her magic as an enchantress or seductress.

The Ancient Greek images of her displays her as a seductive woman clothed in purple with a goblet of wine in her hands. This is the same image we see John used in the book of Revelation.

"Then one of the seven angels who had the seven bowls came and spoke with me, saying, "Come here, I will show you the judgment of the great harlot who sits on many waters, with whom the kings of the earth committed *acts of* immorality, and those who dwell on the earth were made drunk with the wine of her immorality." And he carried me away in the Spirit into a wilderness; and I saw a woman sitting on a scarlet beast, full of blasphemous names, having seven heads and ten horns. The woman was clothed in purple and scarlet, and adorned with gold and precious stones and pearls, having in her hand a gold cup full of abominations and of the unclean things of her immorality, and on her forehead a name *was* written, a mystery,

"BABYLON THE GREAT, THE MOTHER OF HARLOTS AND OF THE ABOMINATIONS OF THE EARTH."

And I saw the woman drunk with the blood of the saints, and with the blood of the witnesses of Jesus..." Revelation 17:1-6 NASB.

So, the question comes to us all, who do we serve? The Babylonian system or Christ?

One causes us to serve the institution, the other invites us into the life of the household of God the Father. The very answer to this question will define who you are!

When we work within the church system, we not only help to promote a self-centered system that was designed to burn out both the pastor and congregation. But a sense of frustration quietly grows deep within us. There is an old saying that emphasizes this that I have heard many times, "Lord I love you, but I can't stand your kids!" The traditional response to this is one of guilt, "you can't be in fellowship with the Lord if you are not in fellowship with his kids."

As a result you either learn to shut up or walk out to find another church. The reality is, the underlying frustration of a lifeless church will eventually bring clashes, as the Holy Spirit drives people in a direction opposite of the church.

A community-based people who are directing their focus not to a system, but intent on growing their spiritually (relationship with the Father), points everyone upward to the Trinity and not the system.

The only frustration we should be dealing with is growing in our relationship with the Trinity while living in a fallen world. It is an unfortunately reality within the corporate Christian machine to purposely frustrate the followers as a long-term ministry strategy. This flawed concept is seen as a way to keep people from reaching "heroic celebrity status."

Cloaked under the thinking of forced humility, it only adds another layer of servitude. Protecting leadership from accountability with the illusion of a separational divide. Many ministries, as we experienced, see groups that should be protected like widows, as work horses who adopt the ministry subconsciously as their new husband instead of Christ.

It was a shock to us when the human personnel manager of a ministry explained this tactic to my wife along with the tactic of deliberately over-working certain mid-level managers to "see what they are made of."

The great Babylonian god of mystery that was brought to Rome is the same god that we will see at the end of the age. Nimrod's dark teachings are still alive and well, and the players in the game have all changed, but it's still the same old game.

These are not the only subtle things we see changed, things that now seem small were once major issues in the Assembly. The issue of altering holidays along with turning Jesus and the Apostles into idols was a big one. All these things are meant to divert our attention and worship away from the Trinity to pointless, lifeless things. It is clear that the early Apostles held to the original Jewish feasts, not as law but as fulfilled celebrations. Passover was definitely a big one as it totally symbolized Christ's sacrifice for us.

The Roman Catholic Church, however, began the process of altering or totally changing the dates and names surrounding the very few Christian celebrations that existed. **"He will speak out against the Most High and wear down the saints of the Highest One, and *he will intend to make alterations in times* and in law; and they will be given into his hand for a time, times, and half a time" (Daniel 7:25 NASB)**

The term 'Easter' is definitely not a biblical word. The very root of it possibly has two origins, all pagan, all of them not good. Easter, according to one ancient Catholic writer, suggests the name came from a pre-christian goddess in the British isles called, "Eostre." Eostre seemed to be highly connected to fertility with the symbolism of eggs. Think Easter Bunny!

The other origin possibility comes from Ancient Babylon. Semiramis, Nimrod's wife, soon became known by different names, Ishtar or Ashtur from which the name Easter is derived. Semiramis had an illegitimate son called Tammuz. Somehow, Semiramis convinced the people that Tammuz was actually Nimrod reborn. Semiramis then caused everyone to believe that Tammuz was supernaturally conceived as she herself was now the goddess of fertility, Ishtar.

And that brings us to another holiday widely accepted around the world, Christmas. The Christians never celebrated it, there is just simply no recorded record of it that I am aware of.

Even though all the records suggest Christ was born in the spring, Pope Julius the First officially set the date for Christmas on December 25 in the winter and commanded the church to keep it. I find it interesting that Semiramis's (Ishtar) son, Tammuz, who was "supernaturally conceived," was also born on December 25 as the coming savior of Babylon.

Although there was a 'Saint Nicholas' born in the year 280 AD who did many good things. The image of him has been highly distorted over the years. Probably the most recent alteration happened in the early twentieth century with the Coco Cola corporation. This last change strongly built a connection between the 'jolly old man' and the Norse god Odin.
Odin is known as the 'Yule father,' here is a small list of the similarities.

- Norse mythology speaks of Norse gods flying through the sky on animal drawn chariots.
- Odin was known for giving away gifts from magical elves who were specifically known as being makers of gifts,Thor's Hammer being one of them.
- The elves were referred to as 'Odin's men'.
- Children wrote messages and gave sweet gifts for Odin to find during the night in an effort to appease him.
- Odin often arrived in secret during the night. And yes, sometimes using the chimney.
If Odin was not appeased, the story goes that children could be taken away for Odin's purposes.

I must thank the work of a Christian Jewish Rabbi by the name of Jonathan Cahn who did extensive research into the work of figuring out the birthdate of Jesus. By his best guess, (and there are many Youtube videos of him talking on this subject) he put Christ's birth date on the Jewish calendar at Nisan 1. Nisan 1 is the first of the Jewish new year and fifteen days later Passover arrives.

This also makes sense why the early Jewish Christians never celebrated it. It simply did not fall on a feast day and therefore was never mandated by God.

So what are we to do with all these messed up holidays? Passover/Easter is the simplest, we just need to walk away from the obvious occult influence and just find fun family ways of celebrating what Jesus did. And since it is no longer "law" and we are under the covenant of grace, families should have a lot of options as to how they can do this.

December 25th. This will require some rethinking. There is simply too strong an emotional pull and that is not something most people can easily walk away from. This should be a personal question between you and the Holy Spirit. Seek His advice and look for opportunities that the Spirit might bring you.

This really is an unfolding issue. And at some point I suspect the Lord will give someone inspiration and guidance on how to deal with this.

The problem of this holiday reminds me of the Jewish issue of the new year. In Israel they have the civil new year in the month of September. And the religious new year on Nisan 1.

Perhaps there is some wisdom to glean from this. One suggestion would be that the religious Christmas would be treated as a "walking away" from Tammuz to the coming promise of the greater savior. The other on Nisan 1 could be a great family time of hauling out our old Christmas lights, gathering some friends, singing some songs, and eating good food. After all, if you look at Jesus in scripture you will often find Him more in a group of people feasting than fasting. So shouldn't we follow His model when we gather with other believers?

One more note.
　Everyone has known for some time about the over-commercialization of the holidays in the West. If we can make a buck off of it, we will try. When you look at Jesus' comments concerning money he sometimes changed the focus of thought to a greater storehouse of wealth stored in Heaven. A place where true wealth was measured by other factors. This thinking was displayed many times, including by the apostles in the book of acts. **"Then Peter said, Silver and gold coins I do not have, but that which I have, this I give you. In the Name of Jesus Christ the Nazarene, start walking and keep on walking." (Acts 3:6 WET).**
　What we expect from Heaven and what Heaven gives us is not always what we think, it is often better. These resources of Heaven are the "whispers" of another world, not one reserved for after our final day on Earth, because why would we need healing in Heaven? No, for the sojourners who are willing to walk the journey, these pools of hidden joy are the signposts that guide us along the way and out of the Babylonian culture conditioning.

My Father's House.
Chapter Five
The Fire of Spirituality

"Alive and warm,

> Dancing with life
> o' they do in the circle of gathered stone.
> Crackle and spark,
> a snap to warm the heart.
> Orange, reds and whites,
> twist and flicker to rise in the wisps,
> guiding the sparks much higher into the night.
> Laughter and Joy dance on the lips
> These are the friends who brought us all to this."

Ever notice that one of the times Jesus arrived after He rose from the dead, He did so by a campfire? He had cooked food waiting for them as he invited them to the fire. It's a warm picture, a friendly picture.

Have you ever sat around a campfire late into the night? Cold fingers wrapped around a cup for warmth and comfort, unwilling to go to bed because you never wanted the combined environment of friends, starlight and firelight to end? "Just another cup from the pot over the fire," you think. Wondering if staying up late into the night will be worth it all in the morning. Ignoring the voice of older wisdom, you embrace that child-like defiance you knew so long ago and stay up "just a little longer."

The Body of Christ was never meant to be divided in any form. But unfortunately the realities of all of us being raised in the church system has, at times, forced a necessary and hopefully temporary separation for each other's health.

I've walked that road more than once, not knowing exactly why it should happen. But in some cases, after reconnecting years later, we had discovered we both had grown and the distance created was for our benefit. On the other hand I have held onto things too long and watched them crumble. So I have learned it's better to walk away and wonder than hold on and make a blunder.

The fellowship that the Lord intended for us was to be ongoing, changing, adapting to every need or environment. And at some point, when our life here on

Earth is no more, it will be Eternal. Sadly, too many of us have settled for the hope of the Eternal while living with hell on Earth.

Disconnected from a daily interactive fellowship with the rest of the Body. We retreat from the world at the end of our work day to our apartment or house, hoping for a bit of silence, warmth and maybe a pleasant conversation before the day's end. In spiritual poverty we repeat each day's actions over and over again until we gather in the 'church' with our best smiles. We listen to messages from a pastor who often feels alone in his efforts, secretly wishing that more of the congregation would get his 'vision.'

The thoughts play out in our mind that everyone else's life is most likely better than ours, not realizing that the common boat we all inhabit is leaking just as much as our lives.

Is this the abundant life Jesus said we could have?

Sad as it may sound, I've got over thirty years into this. I've seen the smiling hollow eyes of husbands and wives 'playing the game' as their children grow up to watch it all unfold. Secretly those kids make hidden vows to themselves to have 'something' better. And the percentage rate of kids growing up in the 'church' and following the ways of the Lord into adulthood, continually drops to lower and lower levels.

Here are some facts from a 2014 Barna church study to ponder:
- 59 percent percent of millennials raised in a church have dropped out.
- 35 percent of millennials have a very *anti-church* stance, believing the church does more harm than good.
- Millennials are now the least likely age group of anyone to attend church.

Divisions come from both within and without, lurking around the corner, waiting for an invitation. Friends separate over issues, congregations split, and staunch "Bible believing" congregations build doctrines to justify staying away from the "spirit-filled" for fear of being contaminated with the unpredictable, all the while whispering that it's actually demonic.

Where is the fire? Remember the fire, the zeal, the passion to do the things of wonder we all secretly hoped we could do? Has the embers of Pentecost grown cold?

"...I have come to a settled persuasion is at home in you also; for which cause I am reminding you to keep constantly blazing the gift of God which is in you through the imposition of my hands, for God did not give us a spirit of fearfulness but of power and of a divine and self-sacrificial love and of a sound mind." (2 Timothy1:6 WET). When we read Paul's words to Timothy, we often read this with the orphan's eyes... alone.

Because that is how we have been trained to think. But we were never meant to be alone. Jesus sent the Holy Spirit to us after He died and rose again to be our helper and guide. Not only that, He intended to be in community with the rest of the body. Friends remind each other, friends challenge each other. We cry, we celebrate, we give each other the 'look' when we do something dumb, and our noses and eyes run when we laugh too hard.

Elissa Yoder - "You be the God (I'll be the Human)"
"Sometimes I try to pull you down off the cross,
so my pride can be satisfied. I'd rather pay my own way.
I'm not a charity case, and I know how to bleed.
I asked for limp, You gave me a gift,
called covered by the blood.
When I was far off. You called me a son.
How can I say that's not enough?

Pride be still. You're breathing all the air out of the room.
Leave the blood in my veins, my wounds can't take away

stains.
In spite of my bravest efforts, I end up needing.
So I'll let you be God, and I'll be the human being.
I'll let you be God, and I'll be the human being.

I need to press pause, so this train can stop.
Will you catch me if I
fall? If I fast from forbidden fruit,
will there be any food for me at all?

Maybe this was never about how strong or how good I could be.
What if the thing you wanted the most was me to accept, your acceptance of me?"

When the Apostle Paul left Timothy to continue the work, Timothy was not alone. Paul put him in a congregation, an assembly of new friends. It's only with the modern thinking we have all trained in that many consider that Timothy was isolated as a leader. I know most of the pastoral leaders out there consider that they are alone and this is 'just part of being a leader'. As a former church planter I understand that thinking, and I've lived it. But what if the fight you are fighting is the wrong fight? What if you are fighting in a system designed for failure?

You see the problem is not that people 'don't get it'. They do, they really do. The real problem is one of logistics. The Babylonian system has so consumed our lives that there is no extra time to give. Forced into the corner, most families make the hard choice of putting the priorities of the church on the back burner. We who are of the household of God have been burning the candle at both ends for so long, we simply cannot conceive any other options. That's one of the reasons why superhero movies are so big. Tt's an escape from this reality. In many ways that's a far better 'escape' then drugs or alcohol, because it at least keeps the hope of the impossible alive.

Fighting in the system, this antiChrist Babylonian

system will never bring victory, and our Father wants so much more for us all. Can you feel it?

There is a phrase, a Biblical phrase that the Holy Spirit has been whispering to me for a few years now, "The Restoration of All Things." This phrase of course comes from Acts 3 and I have looked at it many times. As I ponder it, as I roll it around in my head, several thoughts come to the surface. One is, how little we most likely understand about this. The second is the hiddenness that is to be revealed is more vast that our limited mind can understand.

As an example, consider this same phrase in the WET Bible, it says, **"all things will be restored to their pristine glory."** That is far, far deeper and drips with a mystery that begs discovery.

Pristine means *to return to the original condition, spotless*. Just like what the Lord is looking for in His Bride. This idea the Holy Spirit has in my mind, quickly ties all this to a scripture in **Revelation 19:7-8 WET "...and His Bride has made herself ready. And it was given to her that she should array herself in fine linen, shining, bright, clean, for the linen is the righteous acts of the saints."**

We shall not see the Body restored until we apply the changes to ourselves and do what is needed of us. Consider another scripture from the book of Revelation, speaking in reference to the declaration of the fall of Babylon. **"And I heard another voice out of Heaven, saying. Come out of her at once, my people, in order that you may not be a joint-participant with her in her sins..." (Revelation 18:4 WET).** What are we coming out of? Babylon, but first we need to recognize what Babylon really is.

I have always had the view in life, that the sooner you turn your truck, the less likely it will hurt if you collide with the wall. Making the decision to start the process of disconnecting from this hidden anti-Christ system now is a good decision. And hopefully you can see that may bring a lot more peace and joy into your life. It will however cause some tension with those around you who do not understand.

The messiness of our Spirituality is the direct result of allowing the Holy Spirit to reconstruct our soul. Like a house flipper, hammers and saws remodel the corners, alcoves, and hallways of our soul, so that the Spirit may hang pictures of Jesus on our walls. These pictures cause our soul to reflect and consider the images we see. Our interactions with what we behold in our soul becomes a co-creation between us and the Holy Spirit, to mold us into a unique interpretation of Jesus for the world to behold.

Much of modern Christianity has compartmentalized the elements of Christianity so that they don't touch or interact with each other. As a result, Spirituality has been reduced to "correct doctrine" for many people. Silently enforcing a law of correctness at the center of our lives.

"Jesus answered and said to them, "This is the work of God, that you believe in Him whom He has sent" (John 6:29 NASB).

Our 'work' is to believe, our spirituality is the byproduct of that belief. Our interactions with others, our ministry, is a byproduct of our spirituality. The abundance of fruit, or lack thereof, is evidence of the quality of our growth in Him. If there is no byproduct, there is no evidence of any spiritual growth.

Many corners of Modern Christianity brings a reinforcing, hidden mindset of cloaking your actions as we accept a false concept of 'perfection.' This false concept has almost become like a hidden 'gospel', allowing a lie to fester, glossing over our sins. Many people unfortunately have secret lives hidden away from the Body. This only serves to reinforce the loneliness and isolation with a twisted justification that it will all be ok in the end.

Nowadays the number of leaders with secrets guarding the doors of redemption to their own hearts is profound. Studies from over twenty years ago show that over half the pastors in America are addicted to pornography. And based on the stories I have heard, I have no doubt the number has grown far beyond that. It doesn't honor God to pretend everything is ok, it only displays our arrogance, fear, and stupidity as we subconsciously ignore the work of the cross in our lives. That's isolation, that's being alone, that's not having the connection God intended for His people. This is the fruit of the wrong kind of brokenness.

As I have said before, too much of our Christianity is upside down right now. We have, as the old saying states, put the cart before the horse, not the other way around.

Making a serious correction away from the darkness in our lives is not pleasant. But to truly follow the Lord's command of believing in him to its fullest leaves us very few options. For many of us, the ability to 'share' what's on our hearts rests at the edge of the question, "is this a safe group?" And unfortunately by the evidence of Christianity in the modern world, there are simply not that many safe places.

Planetary Perspective

So let's start putting things in perspective. Let me use the example of a planetary system with a sun (star) and its orbiting planets. A sun, as we now understand, is not just a ball of gas. It is a dynamic inter-collection of layers of gravity, thermonuclear reactions, and magnetic waves, each pulling on one another. Circling around it are the planets in their respective orbits.

One of the reasons we can detect other planets around stars far away is by the 'wobble' of their movements over time. As planets with their gravity circle around the star they pull the star from side to side, making it wobble. As this dance plays out, the planets help guide the star on its path around the center of the Galaxy.

In some ways this is symbolic of us. Unredeemed by Christ's blood we are nothing more than a mass of dark 'stuff' in the blackness of space and time.
With redemption, the Holy Spirit strikes the 'match' and we burst forth in light affecting everything around us. A

new type of 'thermonuclear' reaction starts in the spirit world. Our mind becomes alive with Jesus as the soul learns to communicate with the Holy Spirit. It's through the filter of the soul, the mind can begin the process of its renewal.

Bad teaching, false gospels and traditions make war with our mind, trying to convince us of 'other things' we should hold to the center of soul. Legalistic doctrines, lawless mushy graces, social injustices, unrealistic demands of performance-based evangelism and more, all compete for the center reserved only for the growing life He has planted within us.

In reality, all these things, including spiritual gifting, are not meant to be the center. These are the "planets" that circle around the center that help guide our path around the galaxy. Having any of these things, no matter how good they are, at the center only makes us unstable and eventually endangers the fire.

Due to our cultural understanding of the Gospel, we often lump the Gospel of the Kingdom together with the Gospel of Salvation. This is partly the plan of the anti-Christ spirit and partly just human laziness. It was the late John Wimber who said, *"The church is not the Kingdom, the church is a by-product of the Kingdom."*

As radical as this may sound to some people's ears it is closely supported by Scripture. **"But be seeking first the kingdom and His righteousness, and these things, all of them, shall be added to you." (Matthew 6:33 WET).**

This runs counter to the current mindset of church planting. In the current understanding we send out people to 'build' the church and then find creative ways to try and draw people into the building. So that we can get them to start giving to support the system, and hopefully pay the pastor so that he/she can continue the ministry.

Not realizing we are putting the cart before the horse, everyone works to support this upside down system. A better, more Biblical understanding of the growth of the Kingdom comes to us in one of two ways. One, as demonstrated in scripture by the apostles, was with signs and wonders, healing and other power encounters. People saw and experienced the evidence of the Kingdom and then wanted more. This would then result in building a community to support each other, as the people who often came became social outcasts with little to no means of support.

Second, was community outgrowth by need or necessity, planting communities in regions unknown before. A great example of this would be in Acts 8 when the Body was scattered by persecution. Another example was the building of the Celtic community at Iona.

"As for myself, I planted, Apollos watered, but God has been causing that which was sown to grow. So that he who plants is not anything, nor he who waters, but God who causes things to grow." 1 Corinthians 3:7 WET. If you compare this to the scripture in the early part of the Book of Acts where it is said **"God added to their number daily"** then a picture is starting to form. There was no evangelistic program, no four spiritual laws, no messages of "get out there" and pound the pavement with tracts to "salt" the people.

The reality is the fading fruit of a works-based evangelism pales in comparison to the historical numbers that the Holy Spirit can deliver. God brings the growth, we do not. We plant and water as part of our spiritual responsibilities. God won't do our job, so we should not do His. If the Father brings growth supernaturally or by spiritual gifting this should be a sign to the community of his favor.

By the numbers.

The statistics given by different groups over the years, who have looked at the long term fruit of many evangelistic crusades. Have pointed out some disturbing facts, closely looking at the last two hundred plus years. Their effectiveness is very small!

Many champions of this kind of model of "mass crusades" point to famous evangelists like D. L. Moody,

George Whitefield, Jonathan Edwards, John Wesley, Charles Finney, Billy Sunday. In more recent years, Billy Graham, Franklin Graham, Luis Palau, and Greg Laurie have brought millions in. But even the late Billy Graham admitted that only around six percent of those who "come forward" actually stick with it and display any real changes in beliefs or behavior as evidence of a change.

God does not like waste, and having so many come forward only to lose 94 percent of the harvest is bad management. Yes, in the last few decades local churches were brought in to help with these crusades, but the numbers are still low.

The historical communities God built with His people managing them were different. The five fold ministry of the Apostolic, Prophetic, Evangelist, Teacher and Pastor, built, kept, guarded, watered and cared for the community.

When God saw they could handle the increase, He made the community grow as He saw fit, knowing that the lost He brought in would be cared for. The loss of the harvest was minimized and believers could grow up in a healthy environment, who in turn could provide care and support for the next harvest.

Any farmer who loses 94 percent and keeps only 6 percent will not last in farming very long. And by the evidence of our current world, I really don't think the devil has much to fear about us. One of the reasons for this is the flip side of failed evangelistic campaigns. We are hardening 94 percent of peoples' hearts with the attitude of "been there, done that, never doing it again!"

The Fruit of the Reformation.

Our clouded and fractured history with its many "heroes" over the last two thousand years have been held up for people to see. Unfortunately, because of some odd desire to only show the best parts, we get an incomplete painting to look at. History is thus watered down as we only have incomplete information drawing us to flawed conclusions.

Many of the heroes of the reformation who rebelled against the Anti-Christ/ Babylonian spirit of Rome did so from from a desire to correct long standing issues. But the methods employed were unfortunately just as dark and demonic as the Catholics tactics.

Knox, Luther, Calvin and many others all employed the same policies against women as well as starvation, burning at the stake, and beating to force people to "renounce" their evil ways. You simply cannot use the devil's own weapons against him, it just does not work out well for anyone.

In many ways the Reformation was simply a "surface cleaning" of an old house. It changed the living conditions and created pockets of peace in Europe until such a time that the Lord opened up the New World for freedom to grow.

In many areas of Scripture, the concept of yeast invading a loaf of bread is used. Yeast, one of the smallest organisms, over time resulting in a total profound change in the product. The pernicious effect of this yeast has had a stranglehold on the Body of Christ for a very long time. Giving us the impression that if things "look good" on the outside, they must be "holy" on the inside.

Spiritual things cannot be truly measured by words alone, but by the evidence of outward actions. Jesus made it clear that the yeast of Heaven is a symbol of the Kingdom. But the other kingdom also uses yeast and its slow, pernicious advancement in our history has kept the Bride of Christ from her wedding date with the King.

Too many areas of leadership in modern Christianity still employ the devil's own weapons for the management of God's household. Intimidation, fear, social pressure, doubt, sociology, theft, and lies all belong in the other camp. And as a result display like brazen waving flag the true authorship of headship.

"...for the weapons of our warfare are not human..." 1 Corinthians 10:4 WET.

The reality is we do not need another Reformation,

what we really need is a restoration all the way back. Take the symbolic understanding of Passover. By tradition all leaven is removed from the house days before. Then the house is cleaned in every corner and place possible. The last of the dust is then swept onto a wood spoon by a feather and both are then wrapped up in a cloth.

This Jewish tradition is extremely old. The wooden spoon symbolizes the wood of the cross. The feather is symbolic of the Grace of God. The cloth is Jesus' burial shroud. With the last of the sin fully wrapped up, the Father of the house takes the package outside to join the other men. Saying, "As far as the east is from the west, may our sin be departed from us," he then tosses it into the bonfire along with the other Fathers.

With the house fully cleaned of sin, the blood of the Lamb now has its full effect within the community and we all become the new loaf in Christ. **"The Bread which we break, is it not a symbol of our joint-participation in the body of Christ? Seeing that there is one loaf of bread, we, the many, are one body, for we all share with one another in eating from the one aforementioned loaf of bread." (1 Corinthians 10:16-17 WET).**

Previous generations of reformers have often acted like the kings in the old testament. After the passing of David and his son Solomon, the kingdom, like our present christian body, was broken up. Many of these leaders rose up to bring reformation to the land. But, unfortunately, like so many of the Old Testament kings they left the high places alone and Baal, Ashtoreth, and Moloch simply waited, grew stronger, and eventually reclaimed the land.

So what are we looking for? A new set of leaders to build buildings? Captivate our minds with outstanding preaching? I've come to the revolutionary thought that preaching is a bit overrated. It's not a talisman and you can't preach back the evils of the world from invading your space. The thing that's really needed now in this world is a changed life. Set apart, Holy, and not captivated by the wine of the world.

Iona ~ "Divine Presence"
"Your divine presence With me
I wish this wind could carry words to me
To tell You what is in my mind
But deep within my soul Your Spirit speaks
With words that I could never find."

In the steps before Passover we see that the effort to clean lays at the feet of the ones who live in the household. We must clean and place it all on Christ so that the Father can take it away. Once sin is out of the common unity of our family, we will start seeing the full effect of what Christ's blood can really do.

What is the Assembly?
The very word that was unfortunately, badly interpreted as 'church' instead of Assembly is in my mind a compound of thoughts. Ekklēsia or Ecclesia is a compound word meaning the 'called out ones' or even the gathering (assembly) of the called out special ones. All are possible interpretations depending on who you read. Regardless, it displays a more profound desire of the Father's heart towards us than we have traditionally been given.

The question of why may be hinted at when we look at the Creator and His actions. Community (Common-unity) begins in the heart of God itself. At the very core of His nature is the inseparable blend of three in one, forever in unity, forever in fellowship with Himself.

Self-sufficient in all things, including love, God created man. **"Then God said, "Let Us make man in Our image, according to Our likeness; and let them rule over the fish of the sea and over the birds of the sky and over the cattle and over all the earth, and over every creeping thing that creeps on the earth." (Genesis 1:26 NASB).**

Our "likeness" is a reflection of His image and together we walked as friends in the garden. God could have left it at that, because it is implied in the ancient language that we were "artistically created." But even with all this, God knew we were still alone, so he artistically created Eve to be with Adam. Now mankind was in community with itself and the Trinity, as a reflection of the common unity with God.

I do believe we see a hint of God's compassion toward us after the fall when he told Adam and Eve to multiply. God and Man could no longer remain at the same level of fellowship they once had. So, caring for His creation, He knew they needed more to fellowship with.

Centuries came and went. Wars, death, floods, earthquakes, nasty rulers all took their toll. Many times God had to be very firm with His creation until He took Himself and created Jesus as the promised Messiah.

We all know the story, Jesus grew up and was tempted in all things just like us. But by taking on our sin at the cross, a door was opened for us to enter. Let's step back and take a slightly different look at this, God who is self-sufficient desired to resume the fellowship, the common-unity He once had with man. **"No longer do I call you slaves, because the slave does not have an instinctive perception of what his master is doing. But I have called you friends, because all things which I heard from my Father I have made known to you." (John 15:15 WET).**

Another example of His heart is found in the parable of the wedding feast. The master invited many people to the feast who all had great excuses why they could not make it. Angry the master sent out his slave to gather the uninvited in, **"...order that my home may be filled..." (Luke 14:24 WET).**

The New Testament is filled with scriptural evidence of the Fathers heart towards us. He is willing to move Heaven and earth to make this eternal fellowship happen, even to the point of death of His son. Let that sink in just a little further. The very concept that He is willing to do extreme things to resume this fellowship. Why, why does it have to go this way? One of the interesting things is that God does not change, and the "rules" He lays down are often the same ones He applies to Himself.

Ponder this, if the fellowship He built was broken, that would mean God was alone. Have you ever considered the idea that God was alone? That one thought brings up questions in my mind.

If He was alone and we were created in His image, then does that mean that we are His preferred people he wants to spend time with and not the Angels?

So what is God's solution to loneliness? The solution is a home, a family.

"God makes a home for the lonely; He leads out the prisoners into prosperity, Only the rebellious live in parched lands." (Psalm 68:8 NASB). Maybe this is why God puts such an emphasis in Scripture on orphans? And maybe this is why Jesus said **"I will not leave you as orphans" (John 14:18 NASB)** Remember, the concept of family was created by God not the devil. And the devil hates anything and everything the Lord has created.

As it says in Ellisa's song,
"I asked for limp, You gave me a gift,
called covered by the blood.
When I was far off. You called me a son.
How can I say that's not enough?"

But what is this community and how does it differ from modern church life? The first thing to realize is that everything in this world is trying to divide and destroy the Body of Christ. Because this anti-Christ spirit knows the true potential of what can happen if we come together, in fact it knows it better that we do. Therefore the common-unity of the assembly is one of togetherness. The Common-unity is the furnace, the forge of all things possible, our spiritually on both a personal and a community level expands, for all things are possible with God and we are forever blended as one.

For we are His home and He is ours. When this type of

thing is discussed and examples from Acts 2:44 NASB are held up, **"And all those who had believed were together and had all things in common."**

Unfortunately people often bring forth concerns of communism instilling a slight amount of fear into the hearts of people listening.

But I wonder if that's a not quite accurate interpretation of the verse. Consider the same verse in the WET bible, **"And all those who believed were gathered together as a unit and were holding all things in joint participation,..."** Joint-participation is the idea of a group of people all working together on a project for a singular purpose, not Communism. Joint-participation is something you often see all day long in any business, military or government.

And based on what I know of the ancient Celtic community on the Island of Iona, that's exactly what they did. As an agricultural community, they all worked in joint-participation for the self-sufficiency of the missionary community.

As a result the community became many things. For the future King Oswald who was of royal blood, it was a refuge to hide from the people who killed his father until the day came that he could reclaim his father's lost throne of Northumbria.

And it was also a refuge for slaves, single women on the run, and for the displaced Christians thrown out of their families for accepting Christ.

But for others it was a high class school, bringing a level of education unlike anything else in Europe. To others is was a place of abundance, hope, joy, music, and prayer. It was a 'city of refuge' where greater levels of Christ's teaching and presence could be explored for extended periods of time. In these ancient communities where deep called unto deep for the people of Iona and the early Waldensian, people discovered the well of their personal spirituality had no bottom.

These places were not easy to get to, or to find. Yet, God drew the people from all over Europe to find these cities of refuge. The mountain hideaways, isolated islands and hidden valleys all became the "pearls of great price" to the seeking. Desperate to follow a dream, a vision or a rumor these became the nurseries that so many Christians craved deeply in their soul and eventually grew up in.

There is a basic reality that many Believers fail to understand these days, "If you want light to come into your life, you need to stand where it is shining." That means following the example of the Israelites in the Old Testament, we are to follow the cloud by day and the fire by night. Because we are in community with God, if He is leading, then it is our job to follow.

In these places, and others now lost to winds of time, they followed what they considered to be the apostolic teachings of Jesus original twelve handed down to them. In the mountain ridges, halls, caves, and valleys of these places, the fires of personal spirituality was promoted and encouraged above all else. As a result, all things were held up to this lens to look through. Things like dreams and visions were not hidden, but were accepted norms as they accepted that God could speak through all things including nature.

In many corners of modern Christianity the only accepted method that God is "allowed to speak" is through Scripture. This view would be considered limited and flawed in the ancient Celtic view. For if this teaching was true, then all a person would need to do to silence God, was to close his Bible. The truth is, God does speak through many things, but all things are measured against His written word.

John Mark McMillan - "Mercury and Lighting"
"I've been chasing God,
I've been chasing mercury and lightning.
And I've been pressing hard,
I've been coming up short.
Lately, I've been thinking about,
What's gonna happen with you and I.
I need a new religion, Or I need a new life."

This old life we have lived, within the walls of so many churches is kind of like a bad battery in an old car, we continually keep "recharging" only to be aggravated on the cold winter mornings to find it dead once again when we needed it the most. This is a far, far cry away from the promises of Jesus in John 7:38 and Revelation 21:6-8. Consider His words to the woman at the well, "Answered Jesus and said to her, **"Everyone who keeps on drinking of this water shall thirst again. But whoever takes a drink of the water which I shall give him, shall positively not thirst, no, never, but the water which I shall give him shall become in him a spring of water gushing up into life eternal." (John 4: 13-14 WET).**

We really need more. And more wants a home to reside in. The toxic Babylonian system often works hard to dampen our fires and shut off the comforting peace that comes from the warmth of His presence.

His presence is both fire and water, as all consuming as it is deep. It warms, comforts and excites as well as dampens the fires of the world. This firewater presence of the Trinity remodels you with images of Jesus to reflect upon. Soon we often discover that not only will nothing else satisfy, but it becomes the treasure we know that others need. **"Do not store up for yourselves treasures on earth, where moths and vermin destroy, and where thieves break in and steal. But store up for yourselves treasures in heaven, where moths and vermin do not destroy, and where thieves do not break in and steal. For where your treasure is, their your heart will be also." (Matthew 6:19-21)**

The binding of our heart to the treasure of His presence is a Spiritual thing, not an earthly thing. The commonness of earth is the learning ground for your growth where your faith is tested and refined, making you a unique blend.

My Father's House
Chapter Six
My Father's House

Audio Adrenaline - Big House

"I don't know where you lay your head,
or where you call your home.
I don't know where you eat your meals,
or where you talk on the phone.
I don't know if you got a cook, a butler or a maid.
I don't know if you got a yard, with a hammock in the shade.

I don't know if you got some shelter, say a place to hide.
I don't know if you live with friends, in whom you can confide.
I don't know if you got a family, say a mom or dad.
I don't know if you feel love at all, but I bet you wish you had.

Come and go with me, to my Father's house.
Come and go with me, to my Father's house.
It's a big big house, with lots and lots a room.
A big big table, with lots and lots of food.
A big big yard, where we can play football.
A big big house, its my Father's house.

All I know is a big ole house, with rooms for everyone.
All I know is lots a land, where we can play and run.
All I know is you need love, and I've got a family.
All I know is your all alone, so why not come with me."

So let's turn now to our modern world. First of all, this book is not a step-by-step guide of how to do this. I'm on this journey just like the rest of you. No longer content to exist under the tyranny of the status quo of 'church life', I am looking around just like you. Knocking on old doors, not quite content with all that I find, I choose to eat the meat and spit out the clay bones of the Babylonian system that have been mixed with iron.

For as long as the leadership of today's Christianity remains impressed with buildings, attendance, and money, the Gospel of Kingdom will always be second. Reinforcing fear and instability rather than the power of Love and a sound mind. As a result, leadership will always unknowingly lead the body to false gods. These journeys always seem to start with a hunger we can not describe, mixed with a discontent. We wrestle against our current church culture, personal expectations, family, friends, bills, and mortgages. "The stuff of Earth," as the late Rich Mullins called it.

The hunger pushes us to see our spiritual poverty in greater clarity as we silently start to cry out for change. In the quiet, in the stillness, the forgotten campfire of our soul starts coming to life under the influence of the wind of our inaudible intercession. What was spoken in silence finds a stronger, more emotional voice as we yell it out in our car or in our home when no one is around. Finally at some point we must make a decision. Do I turn left or right? Do I move forward into the unknown or fall back to 'settle' once more into the mire? **"And this hope does not disappoint, because the love of God has been poured out in our hearts and still floods them through the agency of the Holy Spirit who was given to us." (Romans 5:5 WET)**

Moyá Brennan - "Show me the Way."
"Watch the crowd, turn into strangers.
There's dust around my eyes, watch the blind man.
Won't stumble, tell me no more lies.
Show me the way, where I belong.
Please, show me the way, to find you.
Show me the way, to hear your song."

"But as for you, the anointing which you received from Him remains in you. And no need are you constantly having that anyone be constantly teaching you. But even as His anointing teaches you concerning all things, and is true and is not a lie, and even as He (the Holy Spirit, the anointing) taught you, be constantly abiding in Him." (1 John 2:27 WET).

It should be noted that long before we were called Christians, we were referred to as the followers of the Way. This was the Way of Life. These are the hints of how we are to live and sing in a foreign land because our home is not of this Earth. The Holy Spirit was given to us as our guide and teacher. But the modern religious system has worked very hard to disconnect us from that. As a result, reclaiming the importance of our Spirituality will seem awkward for many. But it is not impossible if we connect with others along this journey.

For the purpose of teaching in the Body of Christ is not for indoctrination to a system or denomination. But rather it is for growing up into the image of Christ **(Romans 8:9)**. This requires a community of sustained spiritual reinforcement and true teachers who can recognize the Holy Spirit's continuous work within you. In so doing, they can interact and help the person along their journey.

Yes, new Christians need to learn the basics and often the best way is to have a class setting to make that happen. But at some point, we should all learn to transition to learning from the Holy Spirit. Good teachers can help with this.

Historical Tension.

The tension between the Body of Christ and Catholicism has often resulted in hostile actions. There have been many examples in history of self-defense of one's home or country that people to debate the validity over. Yes, sometimes these conflicts did bring badly needed justice, but I wonder if these conflicts ever made Heaven happy. This is because the devil will gladly sacrifice hundreds of his own followers to give Jesus a bad name. Using the devil's own weapons against him is a flawed plan. We the People of the Way have a different way to live.

As a great example of this I would point to Dave Eubank of the Free Burma Rangers. Over 20 years ago this former U.S Special Forces soldier became a missionary on the battlefields of Burma. Working in the extreme environments of the wars in Burma, Iraq, and the Sudan, his ministry has rescued tens of thousands of people. If you do a search on the internet you will find the movie that was produced about Dave and his ministry. Near the end of it, after all the wild, hideous things that happen, Dave proudly declares that Love is the strongest force.

The Body of Christ has a better Way, and we don't need (hopefully) to fight any more wars with the Catholics. They are just as much enslaved to the system as you once were.

John Mark McMillan - "Love at the End"
"Out of the gaslight, Off the roads we've traveled on
Down by the wayside, Against the sheen of a Babylon
I've seen an empire
Taste the tempest of a gathering strong
But I found love at the end of the world.

My rabbit's running
On the street hot heels of Rome
My hour's coming to reconcile with the dawn."

The Way of Community.

Any modern Christian community will always be in transition, always changing and adapting to not only those who call it home, but the physical environment around it as well. Using once again the symbolism of the planets of a solar system, we look at the complexity of the dance around us. Each of the things, Spiritual Gifting, Spiritual warfare, social dynamics, management of logistics, education, and mentorship are all factors that not only pull us and the community in a direction, but also receives life from the fire of the community.

It is easy in our minds to think of what daily life might have been like in those ancient communities. But we do not reside in the past and re-creating that environment in the twenty first century may dance us all along the edge of insanity if we try.

We have many factors like state and local laws to bump up against, to ignore them only invites the unnecessary hardship of a jail cell, and how is that a testimony to the world?

If you really think about it, we already have "some" of the elements of this lurking around in the corners of society now. So let's talk the 'nuts and bolts' and possibilities of what could or should be done.

Education & Mentorship.

Today there are many private schools representing the teachings of different denominations. Creating a new private K-12 Christian school or revamping an existing one is not beyond the realm of possibility. In a community-based assembly, the pool of possible teachers may expand with the mentorship efforts from older Christians seeking retirement in their older years. Too often in the rush of the modern world we not only ignore the wisdom of elderly, we often push them off to the side to reside in silence.

Years ago in the kitchen my wife worked in, a young newly married couple were having problems. Desperate, they sought out help, unfortunately they did not do so from the pool of elderly couples who had already been married many decades. They sought out the help of a couple who had only been married one year longer than themselves.

The reality was, that couple already had serious problems and the marriage did not last much more than a couple of months after the "counseling sessions." The last I heard, the couple seeking help split apart and then got back together a couple of times. Both marriages are now destroyed.

When seeking help for such things, it should always be from people who have many years and miles in the subject. New elders, teachers, and pastors, although they may greatly wish to help, should be humble enough to step to the side when they know it's 'out of their league' and bring in someone a little older. It's not a sign of weakness, but wisdom.

Mentorship from the elderly is one of the key linchpins and backbone for every aspect of a community-based assembly, including education. And a community without elderly wisdom runs the danger of being destroyed. In time, there will be many who join if the Father deems the community healthy enough for increase. As they do, an education beyond normal K-12 school may be required.

A mentorship, working side by side for a common goal, is a better plan. A Christian company doing construction, farming, repair, woodworking, restaurant, computer programming, etc can all be environments for the spiritual growth of the Body. And all of this not only provides education if the leader is wise, but also a financial base for growth.

"Delight yourself in the LORD; And He will give you the desires of your heart." (Psalm 37:4 NASB). If the focus of the business is shifted away from a singular focus on money, to a platform of integrity, honor, developing your employee in the Lord. Then your customers and workers both benefit, thereby providing a good reputation in the world around. And that is an education everyone needs in this day and age.

Paul made a powerful statement when he said, **"Become imitators of me, brethren, and observe attentively those who conduct themselves in a manner which reflects the example which you have in us...." (Philippians 3:18 WET).** This one powerful statement applies to everyone, especially the eldership. They should be providing and modeling a lifestyle for people to understand. Preaching is not always needed for the Body to comprehend the larger message. The leadership should always be seeking to provide an inviting atmosphere of trust, respect, and communication.

In the example of the two couples I told about, there are most likely several background reasons of why things played out the way things did. But I would like to bring to the surface something that I think few are talking about, Trust and Respect.

One of the many powerful tactics of the Anti-Christ spirit in this age is to tear down communication between the generations with distrust. One generation no longer has the ability to truly hear and understand the next. Opening the door for one generation to complain about the other.

More than once now I have watched people in their mid-twenties complain with the same level of irritation as a fifty year old about teenagers under them. The fact is those under you just do not have the same level of maturity and life experience as you do. And as you grow older they will never measure up to where you are because you are still growing as well.

The ability to fully hear one another is becoming a lost art. And when one generation no longer feels included in the conversation they will seek help among themselves and not trust the older generation. This is why any healthy community needs true elders to be mentors, guarding the atmosphere so that real communication can take place.

Management of Logistics.

Regardless if the Community-based Assembly is agricultural, rural, or intercity there will always be logistics to manage. These 'Deacons' will need to oversee the resources and have the wisdom make long-term plans for the needs of the community.

I am sure, someone at some point in reading all this has concluded I am anti-building. I am not. A community needs many things and depending on its home, will dictate the things they require (Matthew 6:8). Buildings require care and should not be neglected. One thing is for sure, God is not a God of waste. If He delivers something into your hands, then you are the manager of it.

Spiritual Warfare

Spiritual warfare is an everyday reality. You don't know a person's background when they walk up to you. Yes, we can often perceive various things about a person, but that rarely gives us a complete picture.

> *"Some people will never like you. Because your spirit irritates their demons."* ~ Denzel Washington.

Unfortunately many pastors today are oblivious to the Spiritual warfare around them. And in their stubbornness and immaturity they often drive away the people with revelatory gifts who God sent to warn them. These leaders are often overtaken by hidden witches and wolves in sheep's clothing, both inside and outside the building.

In the early 1980s in that small but growing Baptist church I was in, I tried to warn the pastor of things around him. Perhaps I shared too much of what I was seeing or maybe I did not share enough. Regardless, he gave me the look of "I'm talking to a fool!"

He was not pastoring much longer. And it was not until several years later that the Lord put other pastors across my path to tell me the real story. He was taken down by the very things he had been warned about. He was not the only pastor the occult took out in that area. I knew of at least two others during that time period.

During those years, I watched as the occult sent in their kids to the local church youth groups and 4H clubs. Slowly over time they derailed the groups and an entire crop of youth wandered off into darkness. Today the occult has a very big presence in that county.

Now this may sound crazy to some people's ears, but with close examination of the parable of the sower you will realize the devil always sows his seed in the Lord's fields. This means in every congregation there is someone. This is just a spiritual reality that the devil uses, oftentimes taking advantage of the liberal leaning pastors who refuse to wake up and equip their people. Often at the cost of their own calling and congregation.

The protection of those under us is of the highest priority since we are the living examples of the nature of the Father to his House. We the Body of Christ need watchmen at the walls. Failure to do so will cost more than one generation. And having the mentorship of seasoned watchmen training the next generation is a blessing to everyone within the community.

I want to highlight a story I became aware of in the

mid 1990's of an enthusiastic young Christian girl who wanted to serve Christ on the mission field. Coming from a mainline denomination she was never instructed in spiritual warfare. So on the missions field with the rest of her group in Africa. Their group got to attend a demonstration of an imparting serving put on by the local witchdoctor. Feeling something was 'odd' and possibly wrong, the older Christians who came with her calmed her fears and told her not to worry about it.

That was truly disastrous for her. For it was not long after that, that a long history of mental illness, personal abuse, and if I recall correctly, blackouts happened. The many doctor visits and prayers from her church did little as she eventually attempted suicide more than once. Unfortunately I never heard the end of the story, but unless Christ stepped in, her downward spiral will only end one way.

Failure to equip will ultimately fall back on the leaders as they stand before God at the White throne. Answering the Lord with some excuse of denominational rules or it wasn't part of your personal theology will not cut before the King. **(Matthew 18:6, Mark 9:42, Luke 17:2)**

Spiritual Gifting.

Depending on what part of Christianity you're in, Spiritual gifting is either one of the most ignored or overplayed areas in the body. Pastors either skip over these issues, creating teaching and reasoning to justify being powerless. Or, out of an effort to be just like "everyone else", they name drop, claim connections or even worse learn to "fake it". There seem to be only a very few out there actually walking in any real measure of gifting.

In the broad spectrum of Spiritual Gifting, the gift of tongues is the easiest to fake. Because of the social pressure of certain denominations, all a person really needs to do is start "muttering" a line of pretend words in a group to fit in and it will become the "evidence" the group is looking for.

Unfortunately as more and more people learn to fake it, young believers are raised in that culture. Learning to value the fake as real, the day may come when they become the persecutors of the real, calling it fake.

In the early days of my walk with Christ in that little baptist church, Prophetic words of knowledge were taking place, changing people's lives. Fortunately there was a young lady who was quickly discovered to have been listening in on private conversations, faking her "prophetic" words to people. She was quickly dealt with and she was not a regular attendee much longer. As time passed, she occasionally "gave words" to people in other places. But they were often laced with bits of anger and suspicion.

Years later, in another place, other examples faking it came along. As the laypeople slowly worked less and less in power and all these things shifted to leadership and then eventually to conference speakers. There was a well known international assistant pastor of a prophetic ministry who often worked in words of knowledge before conference crowds. Impressing the crowds, few knew he had a "secretary" hired to wander around the crowd to gather information for him during the breaks so that he could "prophesy" to the crowds.

But today a person does not even need to hire a secretary for such work, as evidenced by some of today's well-known "word of knowledge" speakers. All you really need is to be is moderately proficient with a computer and you can "data-mine" Google, Facebook and other social media platforms so that you can impress the crowd with the accuracy of your words. These people who wish to be "counted among the prophets" are slowly being exposed by the Holy Spirit. Unfortunately their devoted followers will be the most hurt.

There are a variety of Spiritual Gifts and nearly every one of them can be faked at some level. I have seen people that many claim have a gift for leadership, but in reality it was just the administration skills they learned in college or on the job before entering the ministry.

Good administrators and managers are always needed in the Assembly, whether it was a gift or a learned skill, because without them the ship will be in danger. The problem lies in allowing people to think it's something other than what it really is.

The gifts that are harder to fake are the more powerful ones, signs and wonders. The very few that I knew about who walked in that kind of power in the late 80s and early 90s. Unfortunately none of them are alive anymore. But, with the growing darkness in the world, I suspect the Lord is raising up others to face the darkness. These people will most likely face the same ridicule and accusations that the previous people did.

The reason for bringing up all this 'junk' is for two reasons. One is to make the Lord's people alert and watchful of the pretenders. The second is to make people aware that these kinds of things will become increasingly harder to fake in a community setting.

All the revelatory and healing gifts will quickly be revealed as either fake or genuine in a community simply because of the virtue our daily interactions with each other. And that will be the exciting moment, for once the real steps forward, then the process of true mentorship of spiritual gifting can move to higher levels.

The issue I brought up as an example in chapter one of asking an elder for help and having it all blow up in my face becomes irrelevant in such an environment. With prophetic elders who have road miles under their belt to turn to, I wonder what the next generation would be like. Those who are learning to live and grow while drinking from such pools of wisdom?

Historically many of the communities of faith that lasted had people who healed, gave revelatory words, and operated in gifts of compassion. In such communities, people are no longer left as orphans to either figure it out on their own or learn to become silent.

Signs and wonders, healing, teaching, wisdom and

acts of compassion become the norm, providing an atmosphere of awe and respect for God. People's spiritual walk takes on a new stride in a close community of friends as the deep within people's lives now call out for an even greater level of deep within others.

I once saw a strange sight while I was in the south. The facility my wife and I worked at was often rented out to other groups. One local group who rented the place put on such an unrealistic, over the top emphasis on the gift of Apostleship, that the outside group gave their pastor a robe, staff and a crown. Then as he walked through the building proudly like a king, several women walked in front of him yelling out, "Make way, make way, the apostle is coming." It was so bizarre, I was speechless as they passed by. And from the reaction of everyone else in the building, I could see I was not alone.

I bring up this odd moment to highlight an issue. In this current state of Christianity we have many people claiming apostleship. And while it is a badly needed gift, it is one that comes with a great deal of responsibility and personal integrity.

Yes, I understand that some denominations have greatly downscaled or watered-down this gift to a single definition, thereby justifying their use of it. While others have totally removed it as a gift for today claiming it was only used in the first century by the Twelve. The reality is that they are both wrong. By Paul's own definition, the gift of Apostle not only raises the bar of integrity, but historically there were very few who did biblically demonstrate this that I am aware of.

"...for in not even one particular was I behind the superfine apostles,
although I am nothing. Indeed, the miracles of the apostle, the purpose of which is to furnish credentials of that office, were fully performed among you in all patience, both by means of attesting miracles and miracles of a startling, imposing, amazement-wakening, and miracles that demonstrated God's power." (2 Corinthians 7:12 WET)

Therefore, if we have any Apostles today, let then furnish Biblical credentials to the office they claim they are called to, because the Body of Christ needs them. Otherwise, I suggest stepping out of the way. You're taking someone else's place.

Social Dynamics.
Margaret Becker - "Deep calling Deep"
"In this ocean of my soul,
there's a voice that calls and calls.
Calls to You night and day,
using words I can not say.
They are,
Words of waiting, words of want,
without You, I'm undone."

One of the purposes of the community is to be the refuge home for those displaced by their decision to follow Christ. And in so doing people will grow and the community will become very diverse. As a result in all of these common social interactions, hopefully people will start to realize just how to truly become "my brother's keeper."

Past groups failed in doing this by mandating codes and rules of order. But that's hypocritical when you consider that Paul made it clear in his letters that we are not called to follow the Law, but Grace. There should be no need for signed covenants between family members if the Holy Spirit is your administrator.

If bad things start manifesting themselves, then that is evidence of something wrong on the spiritual level and should be investigated. There is no need for more rules that punish or restrict the assembly for the actions of the few. All these things should help facilitate and not hinder the growth of personal spirituality. Our personal, ever-growing depth as we interact with the community of the Trinity becomes our outward expression that blends with others. Providing a more healthy platform for the testing of all spiritual dynamics.

Prophetic words are no longer judged in a simple black

and white formula like some binary computer system of yes or no. Now we start to look at things in a format of grace mixed with the gift of interpretation of spirits, thereby helping to understand the maturity process of growth that we are all working out.

The simple daily events of everyday community life becomes more complex as we slowly start to understand that there may truly be nothing one hundred percent "secular". Yes, some things in this world are meant for destruction, but everything is to be warned and we can learn and grow from even this.

Notice, as I have said, I am not suggesting a collection of rules. For the social interactions of a community of faith can provide good soil for the growth of our personal Spiritual walk. And how do you put rules on that?

I know many groups historically have tried and miserably failed as the community sometimes fell into dictatorship. This is because for this to truly work requires people to interact at the heart level with the Holy Spirit. He is the Guide, Mentor and Teacher and that is far better than some social hall monitor enforcing clothing, speech and other superficial things. Let the Holy Spirit do His job and we shall do ours.

For example, say a person does not regularly attend some prayer meeting that you personally deem important. Then there are several possible reasons. A few of them could be, is his or her plate too full? Do you need to step up and take some pressure off of them? What's going on at home? Has the heart grown cold? Has the prayer meeting itself grown cold and fallen into forms and rules? These are things for the community to deal with, not some spiritual hall monitor who stands ready to slap your hand with a ruler.

What is this life, if not meant to lead you deeper into Him? It's not up to us to rule the world, often it's hard enough in this world just keep ourselves in line. We need to throw off, to the best of our understanding and ability, the stuff of earth while still living in it. This

Babylonian system that hinders our devotion to him can be used (because God uses all things) in a way so that we can be changed, purified and set free. After all, isn't it all about who we are to become, Christ in us, the Hope of Glory?

Moving on, The Didache.
 I use the phrase "My Father's House" not just because it's a biblical phrase but also because it's what the Lord said to me. It's not, The Father's House, it's "*My*" Father's House. It's personal, it's meant to be a home. As the song says, "a place to lay your head."
 I have known more than one church pastor speak aggressively against "church hopping." And in one location I lived, some of the local pastors were even considering making a "pact" to kick out and send back any person who belonged to another church. That is a control spirit, not the Spirit of God. Could it be these "hoppers" are just discontent with what they're finding? Could it be the real problem is not the person but the system, the institution?
 That's not a home, it's a well decorated jail cell and speaks of the quality of what they are finding. Home is a place of peace not tension. A place of laughter and joy. And a Spiritual home should not only have all that, but it should at least have tales of wonder being told of the Father's hand at work in the assembly as evidence of its credentials. After all, what is a home without good family stories? Near the end of this book I have included a resource section for further review, pondering, and just general information.
 There is a copy of an ancient document that so few within the Body of Christ know of. According to what I have read, this document was drawn up by the Apostolic council and distributed among the early believers. Several early writers have talked about it and for centuries its existence was known, even though no copies of it were found. Then in 1873 a copy was found, wedged inside another book.
 It showed obvious signs of being "altered" over the

centuries, but it confirmed that some of the many fragment of documents found from the first century were pieces of this ancient work. The Didache (ie, the Teaching) was quickly assimilated into the catholic world after 1873. A quick search of the internet will display a long list of catholic PDFs you can download. Some are short, others are very long as each translator picks and chooses what they feel needs to be included.

With a bit of work, I have tracked down a few translations not authored by the Catholic Church, but by the Anglican Church. Therefore what exists, due to its obvious tampering, should never be put on the same level as Scripture. But to paraphrase a quote from the first pirates of the Caribbean movie, "The Didache is not really a code to follow, it's more like suggested guidelines."

The one version I included in this book in the resource section was translated by Kirsopp Lake in 1912. Therefore it includes an older form of English speaking and many catholic phrases. I have included more modern phrases in various places with brackets to aid in understanding for us all.

This teaching has many possible "bombs" of information that if applied would devastate current modern church thinking. As well as online Christian television programing and how we treat modern Prophets and Apostles would drastically change if applied. Therefore, I would ponder what is said and apply very carefully. I do not endorse many aspects of the Didache because they conflict with some scriptures. But I also see some parts within the Didache reinforcing known scriptural ideas and commandments.

If you look at the general overview, this document was obvious distributed for the purpose of giving some guidelines for day to day community life. And within it, is a section for how to deal with Apostolic and Prophetic people. Let me give you an example of this bombshell.

Note: This example concerns traveling prophets and apostles.

CHAPTER 11
Traveling teachers -- Apostles -- Prophets
1 Whosoever then comes and teaches you all these things aforesaid, receive him.
2 But if the teacher himself be perverted and teach another doctrine to destroy these things, do not listen to him, but if his teaching be for the increase of righteousness and knowledge of the Lord, receive him as the Lord.
3 And concerning the Apostles and Prophets, act thus according to the ordinance of the Gospel.
4 Let every Apostle who comes to you be received as the Lord,
5 but let him not stay more than one day, or if need be a second as well; but if he stay three days, he is a false prophet.
6 And when an Apostle goes forth let him accept nothing but bread till he reach his night's lodging; but if he ask for money, he is a false prophet.
7 Do not test or examine any prophet who is speaking in a spirit, "for every sin shall be forgiven, but this sin shall not be forgiven."
8 But not everyone who speaks in a spirit is a prophet, except he have the behavior of the Lord. From his behavior, then, the false prophet and the true prophet shall be known.
9 And no prophet who orders a meal in a spirit shall eat of it: otherwise he is a false prophet.
10 And every prophet who teaches the truth, if he do not what he teaches, is a false prophet.
11 But no prophet who has been tried and is genuine, though he enact a worldly mystery of the Church, if he teach not others to do what he does himself, shall be judged by you: for he has his judgment with God, for so also did the prophets of old.
12 But whosoever shall say in a spirit `Give me money, or something else,' you shall not listen to him; but if he tells you to give on behalf of others in want, let none judge him.

This next example concerns prophets and apostles who decide to live among the community.

CHAPTER 13
Prophets who desire to remain -- Their payment by first fruits
1 But every true prophet who wishes to settle among you is "worthy of his food."
2 Likewise a true teacher is himself worthy, like the workman, of his food.
3 Therefore thou shalt take the first fruit of the produce of the winepress and of the threshing-floor and of oxen and sheep, and shalt give them as the first fruits to the prophets, for they are your high priests.
4 But if you have not a prophet, give to the poor.
5 If thou makest bread, take the first fruits, and give it according to the commandment.
6 Likewise when thou openest a jar of wine or oil, give the first fruits to the prophets.
7 Of money also and clothes, and of all your possessions, take the first fruits, as it seem best to you, and give according to the commandment.

This is but a small example. And as you can hopefully see many of the modern prophets and apostles of this age would be quickly removed and declared 'false' if this understanding was applied. Also this flies in the face of the modern concept of all the money going to "God's storehouse, the church"

When our eyes started to open several years ago, the Lord had us stop giving to ministry we worked for. What soon became obvious was the Lord started to show His heart for his people around us. From that we learned to give to the young couples that were in need all around us. Only one couple was offended, the rest gladly accepted and we quickly noticed the favor of the Lord quickly increased around us.

For myself, I am still pondering, but generally

accepting, some of the concepts of the Didache while highly rejecting some other parts.

My Father's House
Chapter Seven
The Mighty Three, My Protection Be.

Plumb - "Lord I'm Ready Now"
"I just let go, and I feel exposed.
But its so beautiful, 'cause this is who I am.
I've been such a mess, but now I can't care less.
I could bleed to death.

Oh Lord I'm ready now, all the walls are down.
Time is running out, and I wanna make this count.
I ran away from you, and did what I wanted to.
But I don't wanna let you down.
Oh Lord I'm ready now, Lord I'm ready now."

In unraveling the upside down Babylonian, anti-christ system that has culturally shaped the thinking of the Body of Christ. I find that I keep thinking that the understanding of the Trinity being central to all things is a high priority that should be reclaimed by the Father's household.

When Jesus prayed that, **"...they might be one even as we are one" (John 17:19)** and that we were made, as it says in Genesis 1:26 **"...Let us make man in Our image..."** Then I feel that a greater understanding of Trinity should be explored.

We see "hints" of why, sprinkled like seasoning on food all over scripture. The salt and the other spices of this mystery are meant to be explored, pondered and reflected on. Because I suspect one of the main end goals is hidden within the book of Colossians: **"...to whom God willed to make known what is the riches of the glory of this mystery among the Gentiles, which is Christ in you, the hope of glory." (Colossians 1:27 NASB).**

God the Father, Son, and Holy Spirit always is, always has been, and always will be in perfect community within themselves. Complete, perfect with no shade of darkness, this flies in the face of the occult understanding of yin and yang and challenges our modern concepts of true Holiness. One of the ancient Celtic symbols for this was the Celtic knot. A three strand cord, en-twisted upon itself to make three lobes bound forever as one.

The perfect common-unity, the Trinity, is what created creation, sees all of time, radiates perfect Love, Joy, Holiness and Justice and bends with compassion unhindered toward the lost. In wisdom and righteousness he guides, corrects, rebukes, and raises up the least of us into maturity with the gentle, firm hand of a loving Father. With all this and more that is beyond our comprehension, He through the act of the death and resurrection of Jesus on the cross has opened the door for the lost to be adopted into His house as family.

The relationship between us is meant to be dynamic, abundant, and captivating to the point that the best of the 'things of earth' are to pale in comparison to the greater reality of the life we shall learn. We are not only the 'three strand cord' but we are also woven tightly together with Him. So much so that Scripture uses the symbolism of the bride and bridegroom. With the full understanding in other places in scripture that upon marriage we become one flesh! As one "**...as we are one.**" **John 17:19** means that all the qualities of the Trinity as also within us, and by extension, the community.

And that raises the bar on our own actions. For to deal with the lost, hurt and lonely of the world in an uncompassionate manner is a sign of an unchanged heart. Making excuses with "fine sounding arguments" for not protecting the flock or justifying their manipulation to gain more money for a project is a disqualification of the office many pretend they hold.

When it says in the Didache, "And when an Apostle goes forth let him accept nothing but bread till he reach his night's lodging; but if he ask for money, he is a false prophet." This to me ties directly to a strong biblical teaching found in **Habakkuk 2:4, Romans 1:17, Galatians 3:11 and Hebrews 10:38** That the righteous "shall live by faith."

In other words, this is a test and a sign for the

community. If the favor of God rests on the person, then there should be a clear sign for everyone to see. Paul was a tentmaker, a businessman. And if you have ever tried to start your own business then you know it requires faith.

Here is a bold idea, instead of the modern Apostles and Prophets traveling around from conference to conference and receiving their income from these events. What if this was flipped upside down, or should I say right side up, and like Paul who did not want to be a burden to the Lord's household. **"And in all things I kept myself from being a burden to you and will continue to keep myself thus." (2 Corinthians 11:9 WET).**

What if these people struck out in faith, built business that employed our brothers and sisters, thereby adding to the community. From this place of being built on a foundation of faith, not only does it serve as an example for future leaders. But it also creates support for them to travel wherever the Lord directs them without worldly concerns or adding to the financial burden of local assemblies. Should not the entire community become a well of abundance to everyone, not a black hole that sucks everything inward to support itself?

As the common-unity of the Trinity and the community bond together, then by this simple understanding we should also see the "credentials" of the Lord's favor displayed in many aspects upon the community. One of course will be the Lord adding to the flock, but a short list should include health, wisdom, joy, empathic compassion, unspoken witness to the lost and needs cared for. For in heaven there is no lack, and heaven on earth is what the fellowship of the Trinity brings.

The poverty mindset that has been programmed into our Christian culture whenever we hear the biblical phrase, "live by Faith." Is not a Biblical mindset, it's a catholic creation that in my opinion is designed to make people feel good about poverty. True, the accumulation of worldly goods often derails us, blinds us, and twists our thinking. But that is the result of a mind un-renewed that has fallen into a perverted love (lust) for worldly things.

If we have the right things at the center, then all others are forced to the outer edge. Worldly things simply become tools for the advancement of the Kingdom community because the voices of fear start losing ground, become mute and displaced as we listen to the well-spring he planted within our souls saying, "you can not out give God!"

"Moreover, also your hairs, the ones on your head, all of them, have been counted and the result tabulated. Therefore, stop fearing. As for you, you are of more importance than many sparrows." (Matthew 10: 29 WET)

> *"A mark of blessing is what you're giving, not what you're keeping." ~ John Wimber.*

Filled with worldly, religious poison that we keep drinking from our environment, our minds are at war with the very Healer who has never given up on us. Accumulation without giving is a log jam in the river of your soul and it should be an obvious sign that you are in danger of abdicating your Spiritual calling as an Apostle, Prophet, Teacher, Evangelist or Pastor. If you, as Dwight tried to teach me long ago, can only hold your Spiritual calling in your hand with your fingers around it, then it is a sign of warning to yourself.

Think about it, Jesus who was in perfect common-unity with the rest of the Trinity did not confront Judas for his theft. Then what does that say about us who tightly hold on to things? Abundance flows like a river from the favor of God. The logjam within Judas' heart was the "resistance" that eventually caused destruction. For the river only knows how to flow, add resistance, it will eventually tear out the banks and destroy everything in the valley to keep flowing again.

Within the abundance, grace and favor of the fellowship of our common-unity is our protection as

Patrick wrote so long ago, "The Mighty Three, My protection Be." That does not make us immune to persecution, for even the Apostle Paul recognized that persecution was a sign to himself and others that he was on the right track.

Because of all of this, us, God, God in us are to be in community with each other. That to me means this is a journey together, not alone. Spirituality becomes, in time, a common blended experience. In our altered world view, we see the cold splits and divisions between many things. This is part of a modern Christian view that the anti-Christ system has taught us. In reality there should be no splits within the Kingdom of God.

In some ways I have always known this since becoming a Christian, but this idea was reinforced in a subtle way with my wife's first boss in the kitchen. Charles adamantly defended the idea that spiritual and physical food go together. As I reflect on this now, I realize that the understanding that all things are one are because He made all things interconnected.

Much of modern Christianity has done more for the devils kingdom of darkness than the Lords. And in one area it has pushed away from God's command to Adam to care for creation. Seeing it as pointless in our modern view because it's "all going to get destroyed anyway." This does not negate our God-given responsibilities.

Here is a quote from an ancient Celtic poem, from Eleanor Hull's book, *"The Poem Book of the Gael"*. It displays the day to day insight of the Trinity that seems to have been common in those ancient days.

> "Three folds of the cloth, yet only one napkin is there,
> Three joints of the finger, but still only one finger fair,
> Three leaves of the shamrock, yet no more than one shamrock to wear,
> Frost, snow-flakes and ice, all water their origin share,
> Three Persons in God; to one God alone we make prayer."

Learning to adjust your thinking to see the patterns of God in all of Creation only adds to the wonder and awe. And in so doing we will see the reflection of many of the Lord's parables and his fingerprints. However it should also be noted that because our basic human nature is to worship, we need to be careful where we apply that worship so that we only pursue the mysteries of God. All these things that encircle around that add the wonder and the "spice" can also become stumbling blocks for us as we fail to keep them in the proper context. Out of context, we then turn and start worshipping the wrong things, like creation itself.

An example of this becoming a danger would be what Celtic Christianity started mixing with. The Celts controlled, in one form or another, all of Northern Europe over two thousand years ago. During that time they even inhabited much of the area around the Black Sea. One of those places was city called Galicia from which we get the book of Galatians that the Apostle Paul wrote, **"O, unreflecting Galatians, who has bewitched you,..." (Galatians 3:10 WET).**

As no words in Scripture are by accident, the word 'Bewitched' is generally defined as; "to affect by witchcraft or magic; cast a spell over. to enchant; charm; fascinate." Paul was addressing issues of them trusting the law and not grace. That something or someone had essentially mesmerized them and pulled their eyes away the foundation of grace of the cross to a form of rules.

It wasn't that many centuries later that Patrick, with signs and wonders confirming his preaching to the Celts of Ireland, changed this island. Unfortunately darkness not only likes to hide, but also slithers in like a snake into the background foundation of things.

Some of the pagan concepts of witchcraft through the fallen Druids slowly found ways in the background culture of Celtic Christianity. So much so, that Jesus test of the fruit tree now shows their declining influence as the centuries past. And the warning seen in many places of the New Testament **(Galatians 5:9, 1 Corinthians 5:6,**

Luke 12:1) became true.

Today if you are researching Celtic Christianity you will undoubtedly run into many spiritually polluted streams of thought. The awe and wonder that was meant for the Trinity often seems to get spread around like a thin jam sandwich into occult-like patterns of light and dark. Leading people away from the Creator to the creation to worship. This is happening as modern writers fail to lack the needed discernment in understanding of what belongs to the Kingdom of God and what belongs to the kingdom of darkness.

And in so doing these writers have ignored the warning of their own teachers, Colum Cille (Columba of Iona) centuries before. *"Who can please GOD in the last time, when the glorious ordinances of truth are changed?"* ~ Columba of Iona (521-597)

Ellisa Yoder - "My Father's Daughter"

"Hello, my name is human, my feet are made of this earth.
It will never be different
let the soft places stay that way and the thin parts be breakable
Don't clean up the mess, till I've learned what it has to teach me.

Hello, my name is river, everything unfolded,
everything unhindered.
This is my prologue, the cliff made to be jumped off.

I drink your water and I eat your bread, I can do with nothing less.
I forgive myself for being mostly human
It's not as though my frailty keeps you at a distance.
I checked under the bed enough to know there aren't any monsters
I know the only name I need is My Father's daughter."

The journey of our transformation requires vulnerability. Too many places in the Body of the Christ may quote **Colossians 1:27 "...to whom God willed to**

make known what is the riches of the glory of this mystery among the Gentiles, which is Christ in you, the hope of glory." But few do more than add talk and even less seem to fail in providing safe places for the breaking and molding that is required.

The Mystery of Christ being formed within us requires a willingness to be transformed, as it says in the song, *"let the soft places stay that way and the thin parts be breakable, Don't clean up the mess, till I've learned what it has to teach me."* There's something about that 'crazy' need to clean everything up, to hide the evidence and portray something other than it really is.

Long ago, I knew a guy who backslid and returned to selling Marijuana. He found a place up in the hills of the Pacific Northwest. Away from everyone he planted a stand of it to sell. Then as it grew and was nearing harvest, he recommitted his life to the Lord. Concerned, he knew he could not sell it, and he could not leave it to be found. Especially since he was in partnership with other guys. Praying for an answer he went back up into the hills to find his entire crop had been destroyed by rabbits. It was a great testimony of the Lord acting on his behalf. But due to social pressures, he chose to hide this testimony. Did he rob others of what they could have learned about the power of the Lord?

The stuff of earth has invaded our assemblies and by extension has forced its way into our soul. Christ's blood made us clean, but now with His help we need to take a broom to the rubbish the world has left around us. We need to learn the lessons of it all so as to help others.

As uncomfortable as it may be, I choose not to hide my past. But I know of very few others of the same mindset. That's staying vulnerable, real and even touchable. Think about it, the Bible does not hide the shortcomings and sins of all the heroes. Why do we think we need to? Can we not learn from David, Solomon and Paul?

As odd and backward as it may seem, this is how we not only learn in our mind that we are of the Father's house, but we also start the process of transformation into Christ's image within the hidden parts that no one sees. Because it is through this road of vulnerability and forgiveness we learn that nothing can separate us from the Love of the Father and by extension the compassion of the Community.

Ponder this, we were creatively made from the dust of the earth. That's the lowest of the low. It does not get more worthless than that. This God makes it His speciality to take the worst and make the best out of it. So why wouldn't he start building in the worst places of your life first?

You see, the Glory of the Lord has a hope, a hope that has been hidden since the foundation of the world that all the Prophets of old longed to see. That hope is Christ formed in you. And transformation can only take place if the swamp of your soul is dealt with. Keep it in the dark, it festers and grows. Bring it into the light and it dries up.

Unfortunately a large percentage of the Body either leans so heavy into legalism that they spiritually beat up people causing them to learn to "fake" a holy life. While another section has fallen into the lawless rut of squishy, mushy grace that so overlooks the blatant sin that people fall under it with the deception that "grace will cover it all" and there is no need for change.

Both are a mess, both are wrong. Learn to not only become breakable, but find ways of creating an atmosphere of trust for others to do the same. The reality is that the lies of fear are telling you to run. This is nothing more than just another level of spiritual warfare for you to rise above on your journey.

The river will flow, the campfire of your soul will burn again. **"...for the weapons of our warfare are not human but mighty in God's sight, resulting in the demolition of fortresses, demolishing reasonings and everyone haughty mental elevation which lifts itself up against the experiential knowledge [which we believers have] of God, and leading captive every thought into the obedience to the Christ." (2 Corinthians 10:4 WET).**

This is battle of the mind that the anti-Christ system unlawfully entrenched around you. It seeks to imprison your thoughts, but the best weapon for this is Love, the Love of the Father and the Love of the community. Because **"Love never fails." (1 Corinthians 13:8 WET).**

"We need to learn how to keep people through love. Despite imperfections, sins, and irritating habits of other Christians, they belong to Jesus and they need our love as a healthy climate for growth." ~John Wimber

The demonic realm knows the power of an empowered Christian community. It's a fortress that he will do anything to destroy as evidence by our own shattered and scattered history. Because in this place of vulnerability and common unity, the Holy Spirit can fully become the intended administrator of the assembly. But that will take more than just gathering together once a week, in fact it takes a deep, rich lifestyle that will often make people run away when they see how deep it can be. Or, perhaps the truly brave will just jump right in.

There is no bottom to the well of life the Trinity has, you can not out swim it or out drink it, for is just as eternal as He is. And the crazy part is that He will plant the well in you for others to drink.

"... Jesus Christ himself, in whom the whole building closely joined together grows into a holy inner sanctuary in the Lord, in whom also you are being built together into a permanent dwelling place of God by the Spirit." (Ephesians 2:22 WET).

War is a powerful spiritual and physical reality. But way too many corners of the Body of Christ pretend it does not exist. Really, the only wars that truly should be fought, are the ones the Lord is laying before you. Many people have a hard time with the harsh realities of the Old Testament, with all the wars God authorized. One of the purposes of them, but not the only one, was to serve as a prophetic future symbol of the need to be at war for the land of your soul.

The personal dedication to learn, to stand your ground, and clear the land/soul from the evil that would destroy the peace, most likely has a value much higher than we give it credit. There is a foolish idea that once we destroy a spiritual enemy in our family then it is done forever. This is wonderful idea that I wish was true, but that is simply not Biblical.

The dark spirits of the land and in our family line do not die, they are eternal and every generation to some degree must learn to fight. Take a close look and ponder the following Scripture: **"These are the nations the Lord left to test all those Israelites who had not experienced any of the wars in Canaan (he did this only to teach warfare to the descendants of the Israelites who had not had previous battle experience)" (Judges 3:1-2 NASB).**

The land allotted to the newly formed nation of Israel was huge. And to this day they have never fully possessed all the land God gave them. God sees a value to war. War changes a person and a spiritual fight often brings a clarity of vision like nothing else can.

This runs counter to our modern thinking, but the reality is that war must be achieved for peace. So this and other issues related to Spiritual mind renewal is something I will be covering in the next book, "The Well."

Reflection.

On Reflection of all these thoughts, a question could, and probably should, be asked, "What is the bigger picture and how does this all fit?"

As I ponder this out, I think about the relationship between the Old and the New Testament. How what came before served as a shadow for what was coming. Then, in a blink of time, the Body of Christ was suddenly born and grew in strength and wonder. It must have scarred all the devils and shook the demonic world to its core for them to see it unfold.

Since then the Lord historically has used various

hidden outposts to protect and grow his body for a future, a future that still has not been fulfilled.

The corrupted religious system, despite the dark fingers that have seemed to control it, has unknowingly been the horse and cart the Lord has used to carry the promise to a future generation.

And like the old story in the book of Samuel of the Ark of the Covenant having been captured by the Philistines and then forced by the power of God to be given back to the Israelites. The modern day equivalent of the Ark, The Body of Christ is being set free by the power of its bride groom.

Becoming 'negative' or even hostile to the old system is not a Christlike quality we should have. And it is just as 'wise' as Christians hating Jews and killing them for killing the Lord.

Each of the past systems has carried some measure of the smoldering embers of life to bring it to you, so how shall we steward it?

Appendices

Jewish Bishops of Jerusalem	Catholic Popes
James the brother of Jesus.	Peter
Simeon, AKA Apostle Simon the Zealot	Linus
Justus 1st.	Anacletus
Zaccheus,	Clement
Tobias	Evaristus
Benjamin 1st.	Alexander 1st.
John 1st.	Sixtus 1st.
Matthias	Telesphorus
Philip	Hyginus
Senecas	Pius 1st.
Justus 2nd.	Anicetus
Levis	Soter
Ephram	Eleutherius
Joseph	Victor 1st.
Judas	Zephyrinus

Songs for Pondering

Artist or group	Song
Brandon Heath	Jesus in Disguise
Margaret Becker	Coins and Promises
Margaret Becker	Look me in the Eye
Rich Mullins	Brothers Keeper
Rich Mullins	The Color Green
Leeland	Follow You
Plumb	Smoke
Flyleaf	Arise
Rich Mullins	Growing Young
Plumb	Hang On
Margaret Becker	This is my Passion
Fireflight	Recovery Begins
Whiteheart	Fall on Me
John Mark McMillian	Wilderlove
Leeland	Tears of the Saints
Rich Mullins	We are not as strong as we think we are.
Newworldson	Babylon is gonna fall
Margaret Becker	Moment of Choice
Flyleaf	Again
Flyleaf	Beautiful Bride
Todd Agnew	My Jesus
Iona	Treasure

Nuggets of Wisdom.
John Wimber Quotes.

"If we believe in a theology that doesn't contain doing the works of Jesus, we will not have a practice of Signs & Wonders..."

"It's tragic to see faith healers get caught up in opulent life-styles, rationalizing their material wealth as a sign of 'God's blessing'. Greed & materialism are perhaps the most common cause of the undoing of many men & women with a healing ministry. ."

"Jesus came not only to bring the Kingdom of heaven to others, but to impart it to us as well.."

"Remember, the office finds the man, not the man finding the office.."

"If we serve Jesus then every act & thought has meaning. Acts of kindness aren't just niceties, they become acts of worship.."

"One question you never want to ask God is, 'What's wrong with me– because He'll tell you.."

"Many people ministering in meetings give great examples of how to take the spotlight off of the Holy Spirit & onto themselves.."

"I realized at a certain point in ministry I could either get a tent and have a great ministry or empower, equip & release the Body of Christ to do it themselves I chose the latter as it was the Jesus model.."

"Faith is spelled R-I-S-K"

"The Holy Spirit is to be the administrator of the Church.."

"We need the poor as much as they need us.."

"If you want to reach the lost get outside the walls of the Church. Evangelism is at its best when everyday Christians take the risk to share their story… as well as His."

"Read the Scriptures to obey the Scriptures. If we only learn about God but never act on what He says, we risk coming under Jesus' judgement of the Pharisees.."

"Whatever God wants to give through us, He first has to do to us. We are the first partakers of the fruit, but we are not to eat the seed, we are to sow it, to give it away."

"Show me where you spend your time, money and energy and I'll tell you what you worship.."

"Only Bible & we dry up. Only Spirit and we blow up, but Word & Spirit, we grow up.."

"We don't seek God's power, we seek His presence. His power & everything else we need is always found in His presence.."

"Find where God is and get behind what He's doing. He always wins…"

Smith Wigglesworth quotes.

"If it is in the Bible, it is so. It's not even to be prayed about. It's to be received and acted upon. Inactivity is a robber which steals blessings. Increase comes by action, by using what we have and know. Your life must be one of going on from faith to faith."

"Some people like to read their Bibles in the Hebrew; some like to read it in the Greek; I like to read it in the Holy Spirit."

"How can one come to possess great faith? Now listen, here is the answer to that: First, the blade, then the ear, then the full corn in the ear. Faith must grow by soil, moisture, and exercise."

"How great is the position of the man who is born of God, born of purity, born of faith, born of life, born of power."

"If you want to increase in the life of God, then you must settle it in your heart that you will not at any time resist the Holy Spirit. The Holy Ghost and Fire - The fire burning up everything that would impoverish and destroy you."

How did the Apostles and others die?

Person	Death
James, son of Zebedee	Beheaded after Converting his accuser who was then executed with James in 44AD.
Philip	Whipped and then Crucified. 54AD
Matthew	Killed with a two handed spear. 60AD.
James the Less	Brother of Jesus, at 94 years old he was beat and stoned by the Jews. Finally his head was smashed with a club.
Matthias	Stoned and beheaded
Andrew	Brother of Peter, Crucified.
Mark	Dragged to pieces through the streets of Alexandria.
Peter	Crucified upside down in Rome.
Paul	Beheaded in Rome.
Jude	Crucified. 72AD.
Bartholomew	Beaten and then Crucified in India.
Thomas	Ran though with a spear.
Luke	Hanged on a Olive tree.
Simon the Zelot	Crucified in Britain 74AD.
John	Brother of James, died of old age.
Barnabas	Stoned, dragged with a rope around his neck then finally burned to death.

Didache - "The Teaching"

~ Note; much of this is translated into what is now considered an archaic form of English with obvious Catholic influence. I have used brackets { } to add a more modern definition to some words.

CHAPTER 0
1 The Lord's teaching to the heathen by the Twelve Apostles.

CHAPTER 1
The Two Ways -- The Way of Life -- The explanation -- Almsgiving
1 There are two Ways, one of Life and one of Death, and there is a great difference between the two Ways. 2 The Way of Life is this: "First, thou shalt love the God who made thee, secondly, thy neighbor as thyself; and whatsoever thou wouldst not have done to thyself, do not thou to another." 3 Now, the teaching of these words is this: "Bless those that curse you, and pray for your enemies, and fast for those that persecute you. For what credit is it to you if you love those that love you? Do not even the heathen do the same?" But, for your part, "love those that hate you," and you will have no enemy. 4 "Abstain from carnal" and bodily "lusts." "If any man smite thee on the right cheek, turn to him the other cheek also," and thou wilt be perfect. "If any man impress thee to go with him one mile, go with him two. If any man take thy coat, give him thy shirt also. If any man will take from thee what is thine, refuse it not" -- not even if thou canst.
5 Give to everyone that asks thee, and do not refuse, for the Father's will is that we give to all from the gifts we have received. Blessed is he that gives according to the mandate; for he is innocent. Woe to him who receives; for if any man receive alms under pressure of need he is

innocent; but he who receives it without need shall be tried as to why he took and for what, and being in prison he shall be examined as to his deeds, and "he shall not come out thence until he pay the last farthing." 6 But concerning this it was also said, "Let thine alms sweat into thine hands until thou knowest to whom thou art giving."

CHAPTER 2
The second part of the teaching

1 But the second commandment of the teaching is this: 2 "Thou shalt do no murder; thou shalt not commit adultery"; thou shalt not commit sodomy; thou shalt not commit fornication; thou shalt not steal; thou shalt not use magic; thou shalt not use philtres {AKA- Love Potions}; thou shalt not procure abortion, nor commit infanticide; "thou shalt not covet thy neighbors goods"; 3 thou shalt not commit perjury, "thou shalt not bear false witness"; thou shalt not speak evil; thou shalt not bear malice. 4 Thou shalt not be double-minded nor double-tongued, for to be double-tongued is the snare of death. 5 Thy speech shall not be false nor vain, but completed in action. 6 Thou shalt not be covetous nor extortionate, nor a hypocrite, nor malignant, nor proud; thou shalt make no evil plan against thy neighbor. 7 Thou shalt hate no man; but some thou shalt reprove, and for some shalt thou pray, and some thou shalt love more than thine own life.

CHAPTER 3
Further advice to the catechumen {AKA - Christian education}

1 My child, flee from every evil man and from all like him. 2 Be not proud, for pride leads to murder, nor jealous, nor contentious, nor passionate, for from all these murders are engendered. 3 My child, be not lustful, for lust leads to fornication, nor a speaker of base words, nor a lifter up of the eyes, for from all these

is adultery engendered. 4 My child, regard not omens, for this leads to idolatry; neither be an enchanter, nor an astrologer, nor a magician, neither wish to see these things, for from them all is idolatry engendered. 5 My child, be not a liar, for lying leads to theft, nor a lover of money, nor vain-glorious, for from all these things are thefts engendered. 6 My child, be not a grumbler, for this leads to blasphemy, nor stubborn, nor a thinker of evil, for from all these are blasphemies engendered, 7 but be thou "meek, for the meek shall inherit the earth;" 8 be thou long-suffering, and merciful and guileless, and quiet, and good, and ever fearing the words which thou hast heard. 9 Thou shalt not exalt thyself, nor let thy soul be presumptuous. Thy soul shall not consort with the lofty, but thou shalt walk with righteous and humble men. 10 Receive the accidents that befall to thee as good, knowing that nothing happens without God.

CHAPTER 4
The duty of the catechumen {AKA - Christian education} to the Church -- Against meanness -- Household duties -- Against hypocrisy

1 My child, thou shalt remember, day and night, him who speaks the word of God to thee, and thou shalt honor him as the Lord, for where the Lord's nature is spoken of, there is he present. 2 And thou shalt seek daily the presence of the saints, that thou mayest find rest in their words. 3 Thou shalt not desire a schism, but shalt reconcile those that strive. Thou shalt give righteous judgment; thou shalt favor no man's person in reproving transgression. 4 Thou shalt not be of two minds whether it shall be or not. 5 Be not one who stretches out his hands to receive, but shuts them when it comes to giving. 6 Of whatsoever thou hast gained by thy hands thou shalt give a ransom for thy sins. 7 Thou shalt not hesitate to give, nor shalt thou grumble when thou givest, for thou shalt know who is the good Paymaster of the reward. 8 Thou shalt not turn away the needy, but shalt share everything with thy brother,

and shalt not say that it is thine own, for if you are sharers in the imperishable, how much more in the things which perish?
9 Thou shalt not withhold thine hand from thy son or from thy daughter, but thou shalt teach them the fear of God from their youth up. 10 Thou shalt not command in thy bitterness thy slave or thine handmaid, who hope in the same God, lest they cease to fear the God who is over you both; for he comes not to call men with respect of persons, but those whom the Spirit has prepared. 11 But do you who are slaves be subject to your master, as to God's representative, in reverence and fear.
12 Thou shalt hate all hypocrisy, and everything that is not pleasing to the Lord. 13 Thou shalt not forsake the commandments of the Lord, but thou shalt keep what thou didst receive, "adding nothing to it and taking nothing away."
14 In the congregation thou shalt confess thy transgressions, and thou shalt not betake thyself to prayer with an evil conscience. This is the Way of Life.

CHAPTER 5
The Way of Death
1 But the Way of Death is this: First of all, it is wicked and full of cursing, murders, adulteries, lusts, fornications, thefts, idolatries, witchcrafts, charms, robberies, false witness, hypocrisies, a double heart, fraud, pride, malice, stubbornness, covetousness, foul speech, jealousy, impudence, haughtiness, boastfulness. 2 Persecutors of the good, haters of truth, lovers of lies, knowing not the reward of righteousness, not cleaving to the good nor to righteous judgment, spending wakeful nights not for good but for wickedness, from whom meekness and patience is far, lovers of vanity, following after reward, unmerciful to the poor, not working for him who is oppressed with toil, without knowledge of him who made them, murderers of children, corrupters of God's creatures, turning away the needy, oppressing the distressed, advocates of the rich, unjust judges of the poor, altogether sinful; may ye

be delivered, my children, from all these.

CHAPTER 6
Final exhortation -- Food, and `things offered to idols.'
1 See "that no one make thee to err" from this Way of the teaching, for he teaches thee without God. 2 For if thou canst bear the whole yoke of the Lord, thou wilt be perfect, but if thou canst not, do what thou canst. 3 And concerning food, bear what thou canst, but keep strictly from that which is offered to idols, for it is the worship of dead gods.

CHAPTER 7
Baptism
1 Concerning baptism, baptize thus: Having first rehearsed all these things, "baptize, in the Name of the Father and of the Son and of the Holy Spirit," in running water; 2 but if thou hast no running water, baptize in other water, and if thou canst not in cold, then in warm. 3 But if thou hast neither, pour water three times on the head "in the Name of the Father, Son and Holy Spirit." 4 And before the baptism let the baptizer and him who is to be baptized fast, and any others who are able. And thou shalt bid him who is to be baptized to fast one or two days before.

CHAPTER 8
Fasting -- Prayers
1 Let not your fasts be with the hypocrites, for they fast on Mondays and Thursdays, but do you fast on Wednesdays and Fridays.
2 And do not pray as the hypocrites, but as the Lord commanded in his Gospel, pray thus: "Our Father, who art in Heaven, hallowed be thy Name, thy Kingdom come, thy will be done, as in Heaven so also upon earth; give us to-day our daily bread, and forgive us our debt as we forgive our debtors, and lead us not into trial, but deliver us from the Evil One, for thine is the power and

the glory for ever." 3 Pray thus three times a day.

CHAPTER 9
The Eucharist {AKA - Communion}-- The Cup -- The Bread

1 And concerning the Eucharist, hold Eucharist thus: 2 First concerning the Cup, "We give thanks to thee, our Father, for the Holy Vine of David thy child, which, thou didst make known to us through Jesus thy child; to thee be glory for ever."
3 And concerning the broken Bread: "We give thee thanks, our Father, for the life and knowledge which thou didst make known to us through Jesus thy Child. To thee be glory for ever.
4 As this broken bread was scattered upon the mountains, but was brought together and became one, so let thy Church be gathered together from the ends of the earth into thy Kingdom, for thine is the glory and the power through Jesus Christ for ever."
5 But let none eat or drink of your Eucharist except those who have been baptised in the Lord's Name. For concerning this also did the Lord say, "Give not that which is holy to the dogs."

CHAPTER 10
The final prayer in the Eucharist {AKA - Communion}

1 But after you are satisfied with food, thus give thanks: 2 "We give thanks to thee, O Holy Father, for thy Holy Name which thou didst make to tabernacle in our hearts, and for the knowledge and faith and immortality which thou didst make known to us through Jesus thy Child. To thee be glory for ever. 3 Thou, Lord Almighty, didst create all things for thy Name's sake, and didst give food and drink to men for their enjoyment, that they might give thanks to thee, but us hast thou blessed with spiritual food and drink and eternal light through thy Child. 4 Above all we give thanks to thee for that thou art mighty. To thee be glory for ever.

5 Remember, Lord, thy Church, to deliver it from all evil and to make it perfect in thy love, and gather it together in its holiness from the four winds to thy kingdom which thou hast prepared for it. For thine is the power and the glory for ever. 6 Let grace come and let this world pass away. Hosannah to the God of David. If any man be holy, let him come! if any man be not, let him repent: Maranatha, Amen."
7 But suffer the prophets to hold Eucharist as they will.
8 -- none --

CHAPTER 11
Traveling teachers -- Apostles -- Prophets
1 Whosoever then comes and teaches you all these things aforesaid, receive him. 2 But if the teacher himself be perverted and teach another doctrine to destroy these things, do not listen to him, but if his teaching be for the increase of righteousness and knowledge of the Lord, receive him as the Lord.
3 And concerning the Apostles and Prophets, act thus according to the ordinance of the Gospel. 4 Let every Apostle who comes to you be received as the Lord, 5 but let him not stay more than one day, or if need be a second as well; but if he stay three days, he is a false prophet. 6 And when an Apostle goes forth let him accept nothing but bread till he reach his night's lodging; but if he ask for money, he is a false prophet.
7 Do not test or examine any prophet who is speaking in a spirit, "for every sin shall be forgiven, but this sin shall not be forgiven." 8 But not everyone who speaks in a spirit is a prophet, except he have the behavior of the Lord. From his behavior, then, the false prophet and the true prophet shall be known.
9 And no prophet who orders a meal in a spirit shall eat of it: otherwise he is a false prophet. 10 And every prophet who teaches the truth, if he do not what he teaches, is a false prophet.
11 But no prophet who has been tried and is genuine, though he enact a worldly mystery of the Church, if he

teach not others to do what he does himself, shall be judged by you: for he has his judgment with God, for so also did the prophets of old. 12 But whosoever shall say in a spirit `Give me money, or something else,' you shall not listen to him; but if he tells you to give on behalf of others in want, let none judge him.

CHAPTER 12
Traveling Christians
1 Let everyone who "comes in the Name of the Lord" be received; but when you have tested him you shall know him, for you shall have understanding of true and false.
2 If he who comes is a traveller, help him as much as you can, but he shall not remain with you more than two days, or, if need be, three.
3 And if he wishes to settle among you and has a craft, let him work for his bread. 4 But if he has no craft provide for him according to your understanding, so that no man shall live among you in idleness because he is a Christian. 5 But if he will not do so, he is making traffic of Christ; beware of such.

CHAPTER 13
Prophets who desire to remain -- Their payment by first fruits
1 But every true prophet who wishes to settle among you is "worthy of his food." 2 Likewise a true teacher is himself worthy, like the workman, of his food. 3 Therefore thou shalt take the first fruit of the produce of the winepress and of the threshing-floor and of oxen and sheep, and shalt give them as the first fruits to the prophets, for they are your high priests.
4 But if you have not a prophet, give to the poor.
5 If thou makest bread, take the first fruits, and give it according to the commandment. 6 Likewise when thou openest a jar of wine or oil, give the first fruits to the prophets. 7 Of money also and clothes, and of all your possessions, take the first fruits, as it seem best to you, and give according to the commandment.

CHAPTER 14
The Sunday worship
1 On the Lord's Day of the Lord come together, break bread and hold Eucharist, after confessing your transgressions that your offering may be pure; 2 but let none who has a quarrel with his fellow join in your meeting until they be reconciled, that your sacrifice be not defiled. 3 For this is that which was spoken by the Lord, "In every place and time offer me a pure sacrifice, for I am a great king," saith the Lord, "and my name is wonderful among the heathen."

CHAPTER 15
Bishops and Deacons -- Mutual reproofs
1 Appoint therefore for yourselves bishops and deacons worthy of the Lord, meek men, and not lovers of money, and truthful and approved, for they also minister to you the ministry of the prophets and teachers. 2 Therefore do not despise them, for they are your honorable men together with the prophets and teachers.
3 And reprove one another not in wrath but in peace as you find in the Gospel, and let none speak with any who has done a wrong to his neighbor, nor let him hear a word from you until he repents. 4 But your prayers and alms and all your acts perform as ye find in the Gospel of our Lord.

CHAPTER 16
Warning that the end is at hand
1 "Watch" over your life: "let your lamps" be not quenched "and your loins" be not ungirded, but be "ready," for ye know not "the hour in which our Lord cometh." 2 But be frequently gathered together seeking the things which are profitable for your souls, for the whole time of your faith shall not profit you except ye be found perfect at the last time; 3 for in the last days the false prophets and the corrupters shall be multiplied, and the sheep shall be turned into wolves,

and love shall change to hate; 4 for as lawlessness increaseth they shall hate one another and persecute and betray, and then shall appear the deceiver of the world as a Son of God, and shall do signs and wonders and the earth shall be given over into his hands and he shall commit iniquities which have never been since the world began.

5 Then shall the creation of mankind come to the fiery trial and "many shall be offended" and be lost, but "they who endure" in their faith "shall be saved" by the curse itself. 6 And "then shall appear the signs" of the truth. First the sign spread out in Heaven, then the sign of the sound of the trumpet, and thirdly the resurrection of the dead: 7 but not of all the dead, but as it was said, "The Lord shall come and all his saints with him." 8 Then shall the world "see the Lord coming on the clouds of Heaven."

"Breadstone Publishing is a new ministry minded publishing company centered around identifying and raising up younger content creators in a Holy Spirit led Community. So that a new generation can lead the next.

Our intent is to give back to the Body so that the Body grows like a garden in the middle of this wasteland we all call home."

Questions to Ponder

This is a simple collection of questions for the purpose of creating dialouge.

1. What were your thoughts before reading the book and now after reading it?

2. Do you belive that Jesus has a higher purpose for his Body than what we have seen in the past?

3. Review Psalm 115:16. Do you think we, the Body of Christ are aware of what his role and our role is in the world? Do you think we have ever abandoned our role?

4. Ponder Luke 11:33-36, Historically has the Body been more dark, or more Light?

5. If you must earn and maintain your Father in Heavens love, then is it truly Love?

6. Is the primary role of the five fold ministry (Apostles, Prophets, Pastors Teachers and Evanglists) to control peoples lives, instilling fear or to represent the Great Physician (Mark 2:15-17) and set them free?

7. If Jesus came to set the captives free, then why do so many leaders create an atmosphere of Legalism, Stress, Depression and Anxiety?

8. The religious leaders of Jesus day knew the scriptures and kept the law. But they could not relate to Jesus message. In measuring the fruit of ministries today, do you think the spirit of the Pharisees still works today?

Want just a little more? Scan the QR code below to enjoy this music featured on Spotify

www.ingramcontent.com/pod-product-compliance
Lightning Source LLC
Chambersburg PA
CBHW030301100526
44590CB00012B/473